GREAT LIVES

Louis XIV

OVERLEAF LEFT Louis in full regalia.
Painting by Rigoma.
RIGHT The bust of Louis by Bernini
at Versailles.

GREAT LIVES

Louis XIV

Joanna Richardson

Introduction by Elizabeth Longford

Book Club Associates London

House editor Mark Amory
Art editor Andrew Shoolbred
Layout by Margaret Downing
Filmset by Keyspools Ltd, Golborne, Lancs
Printed Offset Litho in Great Britain by Cox & Wyman Ltd, London, Fakenham and Reading

Contents

Introduction *7*
1 The Child King *10*
2 The Task of Kingship *36*
3 Versailles *64*
4 The State of the Nation *98*
5 The Age of Classicism *124*
6 The Years of Conquest *154*
7 The Years of Decline *192*
8 The Century of Louis XIV *212*
Further Reading *223*
List of Illustrations *226*
Index *229*

Introduction

FEW CAN CONTEMPLATE THE Grand Monarch with total composure. A thrill of enchantment will be the response of some, while others feel a shiver of repugnance. The wretchedness of his subjects at the end of his wars, and after the longest of reigns, was appalling. His brand of intolerant and superstitious religion led directly to the anti-clerical 'philosophers' of the next century. They in turn helped to make the French Revolution inevitable. It was still the descendants of the Grand Monarch whom Europe was to see reeling from their thrones in 1830 and again in 1848 – those latter-day Bourbons who had learned nothing and forgotten nothing.

Nevertheless, Louis XIV bequeathed a legacy of brilliance which only the most bigoted Puritan could fail to find memorable. Joanna Richardson, steeped as she is in French history and literature, surveys the *Grand Siècle,* if not on her knees – as Louis would have thought only proper – at any rate with unstinted admiration and zest. Admittedly, Louis XIV did not generate all the radiance himself. His most solid endowments were unflagging diligence, superb kingly dignity and a gift for saying the right thing; he also had a quite remarkable talent for cultivating grandeur, and for dedicating himself to his own destiny. He might have been, however, a mere ball of self-consuming fire but for the artists, writers, thinkers and soldiers of his court and country, who transformed him into a Sun King.

Whatever the King's shortcomings – and he had plenty – the world will never cease to bask in the genius of his sunrays: of Pascal, Molière, Racine, Mme de Sévigné, La Fontaine, Turenne, Lully, Le Nôtre and so many more. To dwell on the last two names is to conjure up shimmering visions of Versailles, since Le Nôtre and Lully were responsible for the new town and the artistic displays in its inimitable park and palace. Here again a fair balance must be struck between the magic which was created at Versailles, and the no less important things which it destroyed: the incandescent fountains of fireworks, against the thousands of workmen who died.

Louis XIV's women must probably be regarded as an appendage

of the Sun King all on their own. So unlike were they to each other, and to him, that they seem to indicate complexities in the character of their lord and master which we might not otherwise have suspected. Imagination boggles at the idea of Louise de la Vallière, Mme de Montespan and Mme de Maintenon succeeding one another in the same palace, let alone the same bed. Two of them found an added meaning to their lives in close relations with Mother Church.

The story of Louis XIV's rise and decline carries a double-edged pleasure. An irresistible sensation of floating in sheer magnificence continues almost to the end; to be followed at last by the grim satisfaction of the moralist who has been proved right after all.

Elizabeth Longford

Rocroy

1 The Child King

NO SOVEREIGN IN FRENCH HISTORY personified the monarchy or, indeed, embodied France like Louis XIV. He was born on 5 September 1638 in the Château Neuf at Saint-Germain. He was the first child of Louis XIII and Anne of Austria – who was the daughter of Philip III of Spain – and they had been married for twenty-two years before his birth.

The event was doubly welcome, for the King and Queen – and, indeed, the nation – had long ago abandoned hope of a child. It was also considered a favourable omen that the nine-pound baby should have come into the world in the Pavilion of Henri IV. For Louis XIII was a colourless character. Shrewd and strong-willed, he lacked charisma and the art of endearing himself to the people. In this he was quite unlike his father, the energetic, sensual Henri IV, who had wanted only the grandeur and prosperity of France. Henri IV had determined that France should be respected and 'that every peasant in his realm should have a chicken in the pot on Sundays'. The Parisians who now celebrated the birth of the Dauphin with *Te Deums* and public dancing must have hoped that he had inherited the qualities of that well-loved king.

Only the most sceptical would have pointed out that the infant Dauphin, the hope of the nation, was in fact only a quarter French. Of his sixteen great-great-grandparents, six were Hapsburgs, two were Jagellons from Hungary, one was a Wittelsbach from Bavaria, one a Médicis from Italy and one an Alvarez de Toledo from Spain. He was descended six times over from Joanna the Mad, the daughter of Ferdinand V, King of Aragon and Castile, and he had more Valois than Bourbon blood.

There was no time, now, for such pedantic observations. France rejoiced and, at Saint-Germain, the new-born Prince was washed in wine and oil of roses. The midwife observed that he was already different from other children, for he had been born with two teeth. Members of the Paris *Parlement* came, in robes, to pay their respects. A series of wet-nurses, stalwart peasant women, were engaged to satisfy his Bourbon appetite. The Pope despatched a cardinal with consecrated swaddling-clothes. The Queen, enchanted with her son, could hardly leave his side.

On 21 April 1643, dressed in silver taffeta, the Dauphin was solemnly baptized Louis-Dieudonné: Louis the God-given. Louis was an auspicious name among French sovereigns: the first Louis had been Charlemagne's son, and Louis XI had established national unity. The latest Louis was baptized at the age of four, three years earlier than custom decreed, because his father was already dying.

PREVIOUS PAGES Louis XIV and the Queen Regent. The young King's sovereignty is already emphasized. On the right of the picture – clearly in second place – stands his younger brother, Philippe, Duc d'Anjou. The Queen Regent is holding a laurel wreath, apparently in tribute to the great Condé's victory at Rocroi (1643).

OPPOSITE Louis XIV in early childhood. From a contemporary painting. His glance is already imperious. He is wearing the Order of the Holy Spirit. Founded by Henri III in 1578, this order of chivalry survived until 1791; it was re-established under the Bourbon Restoration, and lasted until the dynasty fell in 1830.

FOLLOWING PAGES(LEFT) The infant Louis with his nurse; (RIGHT) Madame de Lansac gestures to Louis, draped in *fleur-de-lys*, who holds his brother Philippe, later known as Monsieur.

The father of the Sun King: Louis XIII (1601–43). From a bronze bust by Jean Warin, now in the Louvre. OPPOSITE The mother of the Sun King: Anne of Austria (1601–66).

FOLLOWING PAGES The marriage of Louis XIII and Anne of Austria (1614): the procession passing through the Place Royale in Paris. A contemporary impression.

Louis XIII was only forty-two, but he was suffering from incurable tuberculosis. In March he had recognized the inevitable, retired to bed and summoned his councillors to make provisions for his children. He entrusted his wife with their education; but he refused to entrust her with the government of France. She was intelligent, but she was a Hapsburg princess who might not, he thought, have French interests at heart. He therefore made her nominal Regent, subject to a council of five.

Young as he was, the Dauphin was aware of the gravity of the

17

situation. On his return from his baptism, he went to see his father. 'What is your name?' enquired the King. 'Louis XIV, Papa.' 'Not yet, not yet,' replied the dying man, 'but it soon will be.' On 14 May, Ascension Day, it became his name. Anne of Austria duly went to the nursery to do homage to her son.

The kingdom which he inherited was glorious but uneasy. France had not recovered from the wars of religion. For a generation it had been the battle-ground between Rome and Reform, and both sides had summoned foreign aid. The religious wars had encouraged Frenchmen to throw off authority, they had produced political disunion; indeed, the moral damage was greater than any material ruin which they had caused. If there was disquiet at home, there was danger from abroad. When Louis XIV was born, France was surrounded by Hapsburg dominions, and although the thrones of Vienna and Madrid were no longer occupied by the same member of the Hapsburg dynasty, the Emperor and the King of Spain worked closely together. Spain lay all too near to France, across the Pyrenees, the Netherlands were Spanish, Milan was a Spanish duchy. Louis XIV inherited a struggle against the Hapsburgs to secure the natural frontiers of his kingdom. This struggle had continued for more than a century, and it had become a cardinal maxim of French policy. It was not surprising that Louis XIII had denied his Hapsburg wife the Regency.

But the testaments of sovereigns die with them. A few days after his father's death, wearing purple mourning, the child King was lifted on to his throne in the Palais de Justice, and he recited two sentences which he had learned by heart: 'Gentlemen, I have come to express my affection and goodwill towards my *Parlement*. My Chancellor will tell you my will.' Since he was four years and eight months old, his will was his mother's, and she had asked her fellow-councillors to waive their control over the Regency. They had considered it politic to do so. *Parlement* now voted to abolish the Regency council, and it was announced that the King was graciously pleased to grant his mother 'free, absolute and entire administration of the affairs of his kingdom during his minority'.

It was too heavy a burden for her to bear alone. She needed a shrewd and experienced adviser to share it with her. She turned, understandably, to Giulio Mazzarini, now Cardinal Mazarin. He had been the secretary of Cardinal Richelieu, who had recommended him as his successor, and he was also godfather to her son.

Mazarin's grandfather, so it was said, had been a fraudulent Sicilian hatter; his father had started life as a groom in a livery stable in Rome. Mazarin – now a naturalized Frenchman – showed no trace of such humble origins. He was a doctor of laws and he had been a captain in the papal army, a protégé of the Colonnas and the Barberinis, especially of Pope Urban VIII, before, in 1630, he came into prominence as a papal agent, and secured a truce between France and Spain. In 1634 he had been sent to Paris as papal legate; he had attracted Richelieu's notice, and entered the French service. He had been created a cardinal. He was something of an actor, a gambler, a man of affairs, an art collector and a bibliophile (his library, bequeathed to France, forms the nucleus of the Bibliothèque Mazarine). Mazarin was elegant and civilized, a brilliant and subtle diplomat, and – outwardly at least – he was devoted to France. He was also devoted to the interests of the Queen. Her friend and lady-in-waiting, Mme de Motteville, recorded:

> He was capable of pleasing by his adroit mind, shrewd and clever at intrigue, and by a manner and behaviour full of gentleness, far removed from the severity of the preceding reign and well-suited to the queen's natural kindness. . . . The queen had reason to esteem the beauty of his mind, his capacity, and the signs he gave her of his moderation. She readily believed that he was virtuous in all things because he had no apparent vice or evil qualities that she could then perceive; and although she judged him rather too favourably, the infinite difference between him and the Bishop of Beauvais, renders the queen praiseworthy for her discernment.

Mazarin's influence over her has led to speculation about the nature of their relationship. He was forty-one – the same age as the widowed Queen – and, though he was a cardinal, he was not in fact ordained. Some historians have maintained that he and the Queen were lovers, others that they were secretly husband and wife. All that we know for certain is that she was much attached to him, and, since he looked after the interests of her child, there was an even closer bond between them. Whether there was also a sexual relationship cannot now be determined. However, it remains ironical that, when France was about to make her mark on the Continent of Europe, the fate of the nation lay in the hands of a Hapsburg princess and a Sicilian adventurer schooled by the intrigues of papal Rome.

As for the young King whose welfare the Queen and her

Premiere Sceance Royalle du Roy Louis quatorz
Seigneurs, et autres Officiers de Sa Couronne, il declare la Reine, Anne d'Austri

Louis XIV's first visit to his *Parlement,* 18 May 1643. On this occasion the child King, seated beneath the canopy, declared his mother (seen here in deep mourning) Regent of the Kingdom.

Cardinal guarded, he was already uncommonly handsome. He had large hazel eyes and light chestnut hair. By the time he was six, he was also acutely conscious of his status. The Venetian Ambassador reported that 'His Majesty Louis XIV has a lively and attractive nature, which gives promise of virtue. His body is strong, his eyes are bright and rather severe, but this severity is full of charm. He seldom laughs, even at play. He insists on being respected and obeyed by his brother, the Duc d'Anjou, aged three. He knows that he is King and wants to be treated as such.'

On his seventh birthday Louis was thought to have reached the age of reason. He was allowed to wear breeches and hose, and he was given two *valets de chambre*. One of them, La Porte, was to remember:

> I was the first [man] to sleep in his Majesty's bedchamber. . . . What hurt him most was that I could not tell him the fairy tales that the women used to send him to sleep.
>
> I told this to the Queen one day, and said that if her Majesty were agreeable I would read to him out of some good book. . . . I told her that I did not think anything could be more suitable than the history of France, and that I would point out the bad kings to him so as to make him want to be different from them. The Queen thought it a very good idea. . . . I read him [Mézéray's *History of France*] every night, as if it were a story, to such effect that the King was pleased, and gave good promise of resembling the nobler of his ancestors, *flying into a great rage when it was suggested to him that he might turn out to be a second Louis the Sluggard,* for I used to attack his defects quite often, as the Queen had ordered me to do.

Louis XIV was lulled to sleep at night by appropriate readings from French history; he was regaled with more history during the day. He was now given a number of teachers, among them the Abbé Hardouin de Beaumont de Péréfixe, a future Archbishop of Paris, who wrote a Life of Henri IV in his honour. It was thought to be the book which most influenced Louis as a boy. He was told little about his father and much about his famous grandfather: the King who had been assassinated by Ravaillac at the height of his powers. History (as Louis learned it) was French history; geography was French geography. In his schoolroom at the Palais-Royal – where he now lived with his mother and brother – a map of 'French Europe' reminded him of all the places ever governed by members of his family. The implication was that they belonged to him. His education, so it seems, was simply devised to remind him of his status and responsibilities. Even his writing master

made him copy out the text: 'Homage is due to kings, they act as they please.' Never had a child been so schooled in absolute monarchy.

By the time he was seven, and removed from the care of women, Louis was already devout, grave, polite and instinctively non-committal. He knew that he belonged to a race apart. He also knew that a constant threat loomed over him, and that he could never have real friends or confidants. His mother loved him, but not with the constant, intimate love of an ordinary mother. She recognized him as the King, but she herself was absorbed by affairs of State. All too often she left him alone. He was an introspective and unhappy child; and it is said that even now the Court could discern the impassive mask, the indecipherable gaze,

Louis XIV and the Queen Regent receiving homage from the notables of the kingdom. Behind the Duc de Beaufort, in ecclesiastical robes, stands Monsieur le Coadjuteur: Cardinal Mazarin.

The King's rebellious uncle: Gaston d'Orléans. An engraving after a portrait by Van Dyck.

which ambassadors would admire at the end of his reign, some seventy years later. When the Prince of Wales, the future Charles II, came to visit him at Fontainebleau, they were both so conscious of their importance, and of the danger of indiscretion, that they played together in utter silence.

On 10 November 1647, Louis developed smallpox; on the eleventh day the fever increased, and he lost consciousness. His mother knelt in tears at the foot of the bed. His uncle Gaston, Duc d'Orléans, composed his features to hide his overwhelming satisfaction: he thought he might soon ascend – or seize – the throne. Indeed, at a supper attended by Gaston and his favourite, the

Abbé de La Rivière, a toast was drunk to Gaston I, and the guests discussed kidnapping the Duc d'Anjou. Meanwhile the Paris *Parlement* were considering a new Regency, and – detesting Mazarin as they did – they prepared to exclude foreigners from ministerial office.

Louis recovered from his smallpox. The crisis was over. And then, once again, the throne was endangered, for the Queen became gravely ill. Had she died, the results would have been catastrophic for her children. Europe found itself in a situation without precedent. Spain was exhausted by war with France and stripped of a number of provinces, and, though she was determined to continue the struggle, she could no longer organize her forces. France was victorious in the conflict, but she was plunged into anarchy and civil war.

In August 1648, just before the King's tenth birthday, the First Fronde began.

In the 1640s a crisis of authority was facing several of the European states. There was rebellion in Naples, Portugal and Catalonia, and even the English Parliament was making war on its King. This example had not passed unnoticed by the *Parlement* of Paris. They resented the autocratic rule of Anne and Mazarin. The younger members of *Parlement* wanted to reform the State finances and administration. The boldest among them, democratic long before their time, wanted to give France a constitutional charter.

Since *Parlement* was constantly pleading the cause of the poor, it was naturally popular, but the counsellors' function was judicial, not legislative. Besides, since they had purchased their posts, they could not – for all their noble words – claim to be widely representative. Unfortunately it was also true that when these 'fathers of the people' spoke in heightened tones of liberty and freedom, they generally meant the protection of their own privileges; and, while they deplored the abuse of law, they themselves sold justice shamelessly. This was such an established custom that no one ever thought of complaining about it.

The Paris *Parlement* had, in fact, no legal or moral basis on which to set itself up as a reforming body. This did not prevent it from trying to limit the powers of the régime by starving it of money; it was part of the *Parlement*'s official functions to register fiscal edicts. However, Anne of Austria considered that her duty was to preserve her husband's heritage and authority,

A leading figure in *la Fronde des princes*: the Duchesse de Longueville, after a portrait by the Beaubrun brothers.

and to pass them on, undiminished, to her son. The conflict between Crown and *Parlement* grew increasingly bitter.

As for Mazarin, he was absorbed in foreign affairs, and hardly concerned himself with domestic policy. 'Let the French get used to my ways, if they will', he used to say. 'I shall not get accustomed to theirs. Once the King and Queen are on my side, every Frenchman will be my friend, and if I were to fall out of favour with them, I should have nothing more to do with the French, for I should not stay in France.' Mazarin, in his arrogance, misjudged the strength of public opinion; his disdain alone could not disarm it.

A barricade erected in Paris by the *frondeurs*, 16 August 1648. A contemporary impression.

The name *fronde* was taken from a boys' game in which slings, or *frondes*, were used. Now the name *frondeurs* was also given to the rebels who, like David, fought against Goliath: the members of *Parlement* and other Parisians who dared to question the policies of Queen and Cardinal. The Frondes were caused by Mazarin's intense unpopularity, and by the fiscal measures which had been adopted to finance the Thirty Years' War (now ending) and the protracted war with Spain. Many events in the reign of Louis XIV and his successors prepared the way for 1789; but they were not the actual sources of the Revolution. All the conditions for the collapse of the *Ancien Régime* existed by the beginning of 1648. That summer the rebels took their stand against authority.

The First Fronde was an alliance between the bourgeoisie and certain members of the nobility, and it was led by the *Parlement* of Paris. In August, Anne and Mazarin arrested the leaders of *Parlement*, including their venerable champion, Pierre Broussel. The result was disastrous. The Parisian populace, led by Paul de Gondi (the future Cardinal de Retz), rose up in anger, and erected barricades. The Queen freed Broussel to pacify the citizens of Paris. The gesture was by no means enough, and throughout the autumn the capital remained in a state of turmoil. As Louis looked out of the windows of the Palais-Royal, he heard the mob denouncing his mother and Mazarin. As the new year opened, the position became so threatening that the Queen decided to take him away from Paris. On 5 January 1649 the Court made their furtive way to Saint-Germain; the move was so hurried that they found no beds, linen or furniture on their arrival. Louis's cousin, *la Grande Mademoiselle*, had to be content to sleep on straw.

Such conditions almost symbolized the state of the monarchy. Mme de Motteville recorded that in 1649 the King's household

> was in a pitiable state. It was badly supplied; his table was often insufficient. Some of the crown jewels were in pawn; the armies were not equipped; the soldiers, though faithful, were not paid, and could not fight. The chief as well as the lesser officers of the household, being left without wages, would no longer serve; the pages of the chamber were sent back to their families, because the gentlemen of the chamber had no means of feeding them. The monarchy . . . was now in a short time reduced to poverty.

Louis himself was sometimes deprived of the necessities of life. Mazarin and the Queen had occasionally used him – the royal idol – to stifle discontent. They had clad him in cloth-of-gold and mounted him on a white horse, to entrance the Parisian populace. But such splendour was ephemeral. As soon as he was out of the public eye, his robes were replaced by ragged doublets and stockings full of holes. He drove out in a dilapidated carriage, and he wore the same dressing-gown for so long that eventually it came above his knees.

The First Fronde ended later in 1649. The Second Fronde was to begin in 1651, after Mazarin had imprisoned the Duc de Longueville, the Prince de Conti and the Prince de Condé, the victor of the battle of Rocroy. This new revolt, *la Fronde des princes*, was spurred on by the Duchesse de Longueville; she stirred up rebellion in Normandy and in Poitou, took the Maréchal de Turenne as a lover and persuaded him to join forces with Spain. Turenne and the Spanish commander marched to within thirty miles of Paris before they were defeated by Mazarin's troops. The Cardinal himself, that 'versatile, intelligent monster', was now more detested than ever; and in February 1651 *Parlement* asked the Queen to dismiss him and to release the princes from captivity. Mazarin considered it prudent to leave the Palais-Royal by night and travel in all haste to Normandy.

Meanwhile *la Fronde des princes* continued. Anne learned that her brother-in-law, Monsieur, Gaston d'Orléans, planned to seize the King and proclaim himself Regent. Since she was losing control of Paris, she decided once again that she and her children must leave the capital. This time, however, she could not make a secret departure. A trail of rumours ran through Paris, and angry mobs collected outside the Palais-Royal. The captain of Monsieur's guard demanded an audience of the Queen. Clearly it had to be proved at once that the King was still in Paris. Louis was instructed to go to bed and pretend to be asleep. That night the captain of the guard and crowds of Parisians filed through the room where he lay, apparently sleeping. For Louis it was an exercise in the theatrical art of kingship; for the people it was an experience which revived all their loyalty. 'For a long time they watched him sleeping and could not admire him enough. . . . Their anger disappeared; and, having stormed in like furies, they left like gentle subjects, praying God with all their heart to preserve the young prince whose presence, even asleep, had brought them under his spell.'

On 5 September 1651, Louis had officially come of age. True, it was only his thirteenth birthday; but, legally, he was no longer dependent on his mother, or on the exiled Cardinal Mazarin. Two days after his birthday, dressed in a coat so covered with gold embroidery that neither the stuff nor its colour could be seen, he rode in state to the Palais de Justice, and announced: 'Gentlemen, I have come to my *Parlement* to tell you that, according to the law of the land, I intend to assume the government myself. I hope that by the goodness of God I shall govern with piety and justice.' His mother resigned her eight-year Regency, and he appointed her his chief counsellor; but henceforward he was officially master of France.

His majority did not mean the end of the Fronde; but in January

LA MARCHE DE LOVIS XIIII. ROY DE F

Louis XIV makes his triumphal way through Paris, after the Fronde. From an engraving of the period.

1652 he recalled Mazarin, and at the same time the rebellious Turenne returned to his service. Louis was not only, now, the source of all authority, but he had the best politician and the best soldier in France on his side. The Fronde ended in Paris in 1652, though it continued at Bordeaux, and elsewhere in the provinces, until 1653. After five years of civil war, the pendulum swung back towards tradition. All over Europe, there was now a movement towards conservatism, but nowhere was this clearer than in France. During the Fronde, the country had known very little government; it was prepared – as it has always been, from time to time – to be ruled by an authoritarian hand.

The Fronde has sometimes been presented as if it were a kind of Shakespearean drama, in which comic-opera idylls, farces and burlesques mingled with tragedy, melodrama and horror. It had had its gallant (and even entertaining) episodes, but it had caused endless atrocity and suffering. No war is so bitter as civil war. Condé had determined to kill any man who stood against him, he had thrown prisoners into the Seine, or stripped them naked to die of exposure. The soldiers, especially the German mercenaries, had looted churches, burned and ravaged, raped young girls and tortured the peasantry. Historians have sometimes tried to justify the French nobility on the grounds that it led the struggle against absolutism. In fact, its greed, unruliness and lack of patriotism were the very sources from which absolutism drew its strength.

As for Louis himself, he was not to forget the flight from Paris, or the humiliation of the Fronde. He had learned that the ancient throne of the Capetians rested on uncertain foundations; he had learned something, at least, about poverty and adversity. The Fronde gave him a deep distrust for Paris, for *Parlement* and for the nobility. It taught him, once and for all, that the King must be absolute. The idea and the fact of Bourbon absolutism were to reach their zenith together, and to find their embodiment in him.

Louis XIV as Jupiter, conqueror of the Fronde. From a contemporary painting now at Versailles.

2 The Task of Kingship

On 7 June 1654, Louis XIV was crowned at Rheims. He put a ring on his finger to symbolize his indissoluble union with France. He was now the anointed of the Lord, the representative of divine law and order on earth. He was imbued with the sense of his God-given power. Bishop Bossuet, in his *Politique*, was to codify this belief as a dogma. Bishop Godeau was to describe the King, simply, as vice-God. 'Sire,' said the lawyer Omer Talon, 'the place where Your Majesty is seated represents for us the throne of the living God.' Louis himself considered his function both as a duty and as a grace. 'The task of a King', he said, 'is great, noble and delectable.' His conception of royalty – as might be expected – was that of a Pharaoh: 'God wills that whoever is born a subject should obey without discrimination.' Louis was not only vice-God, he was the absolute monarch of eighteen million people. He was responsible for their spiritual welfare. He was lord of a land called France; he was the personification of the country. He was a demi-god. John Evelyn, the English diarist, had watched his state entry into Paris in 1652, and observed: 'The French are the only nation in Europe to idolize their sovereign.' Louis was the only man who could defend and protect the poor of his kingdom; he was – so they believed – the only man who could cure them, by his touch, of scrofula, the 'King's evil'. In 1653, in a ballet performed to celebrate the end of the Fronde, Louis had appeared as the Rising Sun, wearing a diadem with golden rays. Long before he officially took the name of the Sun King, he was considered as the Sun of France.

He had now taken up his official residence at the Louvre. His *valet de chambre* recorded how the King spent his day. When Louis rose, the Abbé Péréfixe would read aloud to him from the Bible – or, once again, from his Life of Henri IV, the sovereign whose aim had been to ensure the greatness of France. Then the King washed and said his prayers, and went to his gymnasium for exercise. There followed a dancing lesson, pike and musketry drill and a fencing lesson. Then he rubbed down, changed into breeches and stockings, jerkin and jacket, and ate a hearty breakfast. After this, he made his way to Mazarin's luxurious apartments; for there, amid his splendid collection of works of art, the Cardinal had begun to teach him politics. Every morning, from nine to eleven, they went through the latest despatches together. Mazarin let the King ask questions, tested him and finally explained why a certain course of action should be taken. He taught

PREVIOUS PAGES Louis XIV at Fontainebleau. From the picture by Van der Meulen, now at Versailles.

him what he knew of Europe, taught him to dissimulate and taught him to distrust mankind. He already recognized Louis's potential skill. 'You have the stuff to make four great kings', so he assured him, 'and a gentleman as well.' Since Mazarin might perhaps be suspected of flattery, we may take a second opinion. Lord Bolingbroke was one of the few contemporary foreigners competent to judge the King's ability. He recorded:

When Louis XIV took the administration of affairs into his own hands, . . . he was in the prime of his age, and had, what princes seldom have, the advantages of youth and those of experience together. . . . He jested sometimes on his own ignorance; and there were other defects in his character, owing to his education, which he did not see. But Mazarin had initiated him into the mysteries of his policy. He had seen a great part of those foundations laid, on which he was to raise the fabric of his future grandeur; and, as Mazarin finished the work that Richelieu began, he had the lessons of one, and the examples of both, to instruct him.

He had acquired habits of secrecy and method in business; of reserve, discretion, decency, and dignity in behaviour. If he was not the greatest King, he was the best actor of majesty, at least, that ever filled a throne. He by no means wanted that courage which is commonly called bravery, though the want of it was imputed to him in the midst of his greatest triumphs: nor that other courage, less ostentatious and more rarely found, calm, steady, persevering resolution, which seems to arise less from the temper of the body, and is therefore called courage of the mind. He had them both most certainly, and I could produce unquestionable anecdotes in proof. He was, in one word, much superior to any prince with whom he had to do, when he began to govern.

At eleven o'clock every morning, when Louis had finished his session with Mazarin, he would go to his mother's room while she had her breakfast. Mme de Motteville tells us that

her breakfast was always good, for her health was admirable. After her bouillon she was served with cutlets, sausages, and boiled bread [*sic*]. . . . Then she took her chemise, which the King gave her, kissing her tenderly; and this custom lasted a long time. . . . She dressed with care and the choiceness permissible to those who desire to look well without luxury, without gold or silver, paint, or any extravagant fashion. . . .

When the King left his mother, he practised his horsemanship at the riding-school. Then he returned to hear Mass with her.

In matters of religion, Anne was his teacher and his example. She had kept all her passionate Spanish faith. She fasted whenever it was prescribed, and she regularly went to communion.

FOLLOWING PAGES Louis XIV, King of France and of Navarre. This engraving of about 1659 shows him in all his majesty.

LARI
LOVIS XIII
LEMPIRE
Apres tant deffortѕ inutiles
pour abatre ta gloire et pour men reuesЅir
les peines quon ma faict sentir
mont reduict au seul poĩct de cõseruer mes viles
iay toutesfois conquis ceque iay pretendu
et ma force icy te surpasse
puisque malgre lessort dont tu tes deffendu
iay pris vne place en ta grace
I Lagnet excudit

DE
ANCE ET DE
LESPAGNE
Prince illustre present des Cieux
ta gloire va du pair auec celle des Dieux
et ta propre ennemie
a genoux deuant toy s'en confesse ébloüie
quelques efforts que nous fassions
tes peuples diuisez ne donnēt rien a mordre
et ces braues suiectz malgré tout leur desordre
sont pour toy des agneaux cōtre nous des Lions

On the eve of high feast days, she would go to Val-de-Grâce and stay there for some days, in complete seclusion. On Good Fridays she would go into retreat from five o'clock in the morning. But it never occurred to her to strengthen her faith by study. She disliked reading, and knew next to nothing. Louis adopted her blind faith and her determined ignorance. He, too, never opened a theological work. Mother and son both believed that kings did not settle theological problems: they only enforced the decisions which the Church dictated. The thought of religious tolerance remained repellent to them. Only free-thinkers could imagine Catholic truth co-existing with heretic falsehood. Louis was later to find other reasons for defending the Catholic faith. He was also to learn that public piety could absolve a multitude of sins.

When he had heard Mass with his mother at the Palais-Royal, he had his lunch with her. He had already formed the habit of taking his meals in public. In the afternoon he had an hour's study with his tutor, and spent the rest of the time at *jeu de paume* (tennis), hunting or shooting. He might take an evening drive in his carriage beside the Seine. After supper there might be parlour games with his mother's ladies-in-waiting, or a game of *hoca* – a primitive form of roulette. Mazarin had brought *hoca* from Italy, and he did not hesitate to cheat. As a diplomat, he called this 'correcting chance'.

But such diversions ended early, and Louis would be in bed by midnight. The atmosphere at Court was still far from gay. The Fronde was over, the Thirty Years' War had ended in 1648, but hostilities with Spain continued; and Nicolas Fouquet, the Superintendent of Finances, had needed to devise new ways of raising funds to support an army of seventeen thousand men. Louis had signed the edicts, and on 20 March 1655 he went to *Parlement* to get them registered. *Parlement* voted in favour; but, early in April, the Chancellor admitted to the *Chambre des Enquêtes* that he had had no previous knowledge of the edicts, and that he had affixed the great seal without having read them. This was more than *Parlement* was prepared to accept. Soon afterwards, shooting at Vincennes, Louis was informed that, on its own authority, *Parlement* was assembling for a new joint session.

A meeting of *Parlement* without the King's approval was not only illegal but a direct challenge to his sovereignty. Louis was sixteen, but he was already determined to show that he was King. He rode at once to Paris, and, unannounced, he entered the Grand' Chambre at the Palais de Justice. He forbade the members of

Parlement to hold their session. Then, leaving them speechless, he walked out of the hall. Legend says that it was on that day that he uttered the famous words: *'L'État, c'est moi.'* There is no evidence that he did. But certainly, for the first time, he asserted his personal authority.

He had strengthened not only his own position, but that of Mazarin, the most powerful man on the Continent of Europe. Mazarin was now Prime Minister and head of the Council, superintendent of the Queen's household and the King's education (not to mention that of the Duc d'Anjou). He held a number of sinecures which brought him resounding titles and substantial sums of money. He also found time to exploit commercial interests; he held shares in a whaling company, owned cargo ships and had founded a business to trade in Algerian cork and coral. He had amassed a fortune of some £17,000,000.

Having secured the present for himself in France, the Cardinal had long ago determined to secure the future of his family. He had sent for his nephews and nieces of marriageable age. The first consignment had arrived in 1647; in 1654 his sister, Mme Mancini, arrived with two daughters, Hortense and Marie. The Mazarinettes, as Paris called them, were lively, clever and attractive. When he was seventeen, Louis met Marie, and fell in love with her.

She was sixteen, tall, dark-eyed and dark-haired.

> She was not a beauty [wrote a contemporary], but her movements, her manner, the whole bearing of her person, were the result of a nature guided by grace. Her look was tender; the accent of her voice enchanting; her genius was great, substantial and extensive, and capable of the grandest conceptions. She wrote both good prose and pleasing poetry; and Marie de Mancini, who shone in a courtly letter, was equally capable of producing a political or state despatch. She would not have been unworthy of the throne, if among us great merit had been a title to obtain it.

For some months the idyll continued. At Fontainebleau there were picnics in the forest, water-parties on the lake, comedies and ballets. Louis did not make Marie his mistress; but, overwhelmed by his first love, forgetting the demands of his kingship, he asked Mazarin for her hand. The Cardinal was too wise to ruin his achievement by over-reaching. He refused to allow his niece to be Queen of France; and, aided by the King's mother, he sent her away from Court. Eleven years later, the parting of

Louis and Marie Mancini inspired Racine to write *Bérénice*. Marie made an unhappy marriage with the Constable Colonna. Mazarin had already selected a more appropriate wife for the King of France. After protracted warfare, peace with Spain seemed at last to be imminent. Philip IV had no son, and marriage with one of his daughters would place the children of such an alliance in direct succession to the Spanish throne. The romance of Louis and Marie Mancini was soon followed by the Treaty of the Pyrenees, which ended the long war with Spain, and settled Louis's marriage with the Infanta Maria Teresa. The Treaty strengthened France, but it did not enable her to break the circle of Hapsburg possessions by which she had been surrounded since the days of Charles V. It did little more than express the weariness of the two countries which had been at war for so long. But Philip IV was ailing, and France found it politic to ensure herself the Spanish heritage. A clause in the Treaty stipulated that, if the Infanta's dowry were not paid, then the Infanta should retain her rights over Spain and Spanish possessions. Mazarin – who was, of course, responsible for the clause – was thinking particularly of the Spanish Netherlands. He was well aware that Spain was bankrupt, and that the massive dowry – half a million gold écus – would probably not be paid in full.

On 21 September 1659, even before the conclusion of the Treaty, Louis addressed himself to the King of Spain:

Most High, Excellent, and Powerful Prince, our very dear and well-beloved Brother and Uncle –

It having pleased God to bless the good intentions we have had of giving peace to Christendom, and of re-establishing between us in this way the friendship and unity which there should be in view of the closeness of our relationship, all that is wanting to complete our satisfaction is to see the duration of the peace assured, and the ties of our amity and kinship strengthened, by a new alliance which we have always desired. We allude to our marriage with the Most Serene Infanta Doña Maria Teresa, the eldest daughter of Your Majesty, which we contemplate and desire, less on account of the greatness of her birth and position, than for her exceptional personal qualities.

For this reason we are sending as ambassador extraordinary to Your Majesty our dearly-beloved cousin the Duc de Gramont, Peer and Marshal of France, Lord of Bidacke, Minister of State, Governor and Lieutenant-General in Navarre and Bearn, Governor of the Town of Bayonne and of the district of Labour, and commander of our French Guards, to ask Your Majesty in our name, as we do also in this letter, to grant us for wife the aforesaid Most Serene Infanta Doña Maria Teresa. . . .

OPPOSITE Maria Teresa, daughter of Philip IV, King of Spain, and future wife of Louis XIV. She is seen here, painted in her childhood by Velasquez, who appears with brushes and palette on the left of the picture.

FOLLOWING PAGES The marriage of Louis XIV and the Infanta Maria Teresa, 8 June 1660. Anne of Austria is seen on the left, between her younger son and Mazarin (who had been largely responsible for the alliance).

LE MARIAGE DV
PAR·LARCHEVESQ
A FONTARABIE ET A

AVEC LINFANTE
PAMPELVNE CELEBre
LVS le 9 Iuin 1660

Arc de pierre sur le pont dormant de la porte sainct Anthoine

It was, as we have seen, a purely political marriage. Genetically it was not advisable, since Louis and his prospective bride were first cousins. Nor was it likely to prove a marriage of love. Mme de Motteville left a sharp, condescending account of Maria Teresa:

> The Infanta-queen was small, but well made; we admired the most dazzling whiteness of complexion ever seen. . . . Her blue eyes appeared to us to be fine, and charmed us by their softness and brilliancy. We celebrated the beauty of her mouth, and of her somewhat full and roseate lips. The outline of her face is long, but, being rounded at the chin, pleased us; her cheeks, rather large but handsome, had their share of our praise. Her hair was that silvery blond, which suits so perfectly the beautiful colours of her complexion. To speak the truth, with more height and handsomer teeth, she would deserve to be estimated one of the most beautiful persons in Europe. Her bust appeared to be well formed and tolerably full, but her dress was horrible.

Despite her shortness, her horrible dress and her unhandsome teeth, she was destined to be Queen of France. On 3 June 1660 she was married by proxy at Fuenterrabia; six days later she met Louis, and the marriage proper was solemnized at Saint-Jean-de-Luz. The Treaty of the Pyrenees had been ratified already.

Louis and Maria Teresa spent the first year of their marriage in a series of festivities of unprecedented splendour. Their entry into Paris inspired an extraordinary show of loyalty; and Mazarin returned at the pinnacle of his power to the city which he had once been obliged to flee at dead of night. He intended to impress the metropolis with his triumph: his household took more than an hour to pass in procession. The household of Monsieur, the King's brother, followed; and Mme Scarron, the wife of the comic poet, who saw it pass, declared that it 'appeared most pitiable; and they say this was done by design, in order to display the excessive opulence of the Cardinal'.

He was not to display his opulence much longer. By March 1661 he was dying. On 7 March he received Extreme Unction. 'He sent for his servants, and let them all see him; having had his beard trimmed, and being clean and agreeable-looking in a flame-coloured gown, with his cardinal's cap on his head, like a man who braved death.' He 'bequeathed to the King as a principal maxim, to do his own business and never again to raise a Prime Minister to the height that he himself had reached; confessing to him that he knew . . . how dangerous it was for a king to put a man in that position'. He died on 9 March.

This elaborate triumphal arch was erected near the Porte Saint-Antoine, in Paris, to celebrate the royal marriage.

Louis had learned the lesson which Mazarin had taught him; he had also reached his private conclusions about Mazarin. He was (so he wrote, later, in his unfinished *Mémoires*)

a very skilful and accomplished minister. He was fond of me, and I was fond of him, and he had done me great service. But his thoughts and ways were naturally very different from mine, and I could not contradict him or detract in the least from his credit without once again stirring up against him . . . those same storms [the Fronde] which had been so difficult to calm.

And, addressing himself to his son, Louis added:

I determined, above all, not to have a Prime Minister; and if you have faith in me, my son, you and all your successors, the title will be abolished for ever in France. For nothing is more unworthy than to see all the power on one side, and only the title of King on the other.

Never had there been more intrigues and expectations in any Court than there were in the last days of Mazarin. Women with a claim to beauty flattered themselves that they would influence a susceptible prince of twenty-two. Young courtiers believed that they would revive the rule of favourites. Every minister hoped to be Prime Minister. None of them thought that the King would dare to take the burden of government upon himself.

They all proved to be wrong. From the first, the King was the ruler of the country, and his mastery increased as his reign advanced. Soon after Mazarin had died, the president of the ecclesiastical assembly asked Louis to whom he should now address himself on questions of public business. 'To myself', replied the King. A new era had begun.

It was an era for which Louis himself had long prepared.

I never stopped testing myself in private [so he confessed]. I confided in no-one, reasoned alone and with myself about all the events that occurred. I was full of hope and joy when I found that my first thoughts were the same as the final conclusions of clever and accomplished people; and I was fundamentally convinced that I had not been placed and preserved on the throne with so great a passion to do well without being provided with the means.

Now at last the moment of true sovereignty had come. 'I realized', he wrote, 'that I was King; for that I had been born. I was transfused with sweet exaltation.' It was not surprising that a King so full of pride and energy should devote himself to his profession. In his *Mémoires* he later set down his ideas and his feelings. He did so to clarify his theories, and to instruct his son. He also did so for posterity. He wanted 'to put historians on the right path'.

He began his *Mémoires* by differentiating between spiritual and temporal powers. He was convinced that he held his own power directly from God. Louis had always had a deep religious sense. He assured his son: 'The first lessons of politics are those which teach us to serve the Deity; the submission we show Him is the noblest example we can set for the submission which is due to ourselves; and we err against prudence, as well as justice, when we fail in veneration towards that Being of whom we are the vice-regents.' Since a king is endowed with such immense responsibility, since he is the deputy of God, he must always control his emotions, and 'govern himself opportunely, either to stifle or declare his anger. Exercising as we do a divine function here below, we should appear to be incapable of entertaining those emotions which would disgrace us.' The King must be master of himself, and jealous of his supremacy. 'There is nothing', Louis wrote, 'which we ought to guard more jealously than that pre-eminence. . . . It is important to the public to be governed only by one person. It is also important to them that he who holds that function should be exalted so much above all others, that no other person could possibly be compared with him.' He was determined to exalt himself above all others; he was also determined to accept no limitations to his power except those dictated by justice and reason. Repeatedly he identified the royal authority with reason. And it was this rational quality that, according to him, distinguished the royal authority from the rest. The King, he wrote, was governed by reason, but it was reason derived from wide practical experience. He alone was competent to decide what was best for the state. 'It is always worse for the public to control the government than to support even a bad government that is directed by kings *whom God alone can judge*.' No belief could be further from the modern political ideal; but Louis disdained and indeed abhorred the concept of democracy.

And yet, though he was absolutist, Louis was rational. He understood the appalling responsibility of a man endowed with such power. He knew that he must take unremitting pains, and that he must also surround himself with the best advisers. He must be accurately informed. 'A man who is well informed about all that occurs will not make mistakes. A ruler's most obvious duty is therefore *to take every possible precaution to know everything that is happening in his age*.' So it was that he determined to be informed about everything

> listening to the least of my subjects, knowing at any time the numbers and quality of my troops and the state of my strongholds, unceasingly giving my instructions upon every requirement, dealing directly with ministers from abroad, receiving and reading despatches, making some of the replies myself, regulating the income and expenditure of my State and keeping my affairs secret as no other man had done before me.

Birth, wrote the King, should be strengthened by distinction. 'The elevation of rank is never more firm and more secure than when it is sustained by singular merit.' The King must learn wisdom: 'The able monarch, like the wise pilot, should know how to use every wind to advance towards his destined port.' The King must not be proud of himself, but he must be proud of his crown. He must remember the supreme importance of his fame. 'Kings, who are born to possess and command, should never be ashamed to subject themselves to whatever the care of their fame requires of them. . . . Reputation often accomplishes more than the mightiest armies; conquerors have done more by their name than by the sword.' He himself was consumed by love of glory, like a character in Corneille. 'In my heart I valued above all else, more than life itself, a high reputation. . . . A governing and overriding passion for greatness and glory stifles all other passions in kings.'

In 1662, a year after Mazarin's death, Louis XIV adopted his personal symbol.

> I chose to assume the form of the sun, because of the unique quality of the radiance that surrounds it; the light that it imparts to the other stars, which compose a kind of court; the fair and equal share of that light that it gives to all the various climates of the world; the good it does in every place, ceaselessly producing joy and activity on every side; the untiring motion in which it yet seems always tranquil; and that constant, invariable course from which it never deviates or diverges – assuredly the most vivid and beautiful image of a great monarch. Those who saw me ruling with a degree of ease, unhampered by the many cares that royalty has to assume, persuaded me to add the globe of the earth, and for a motto *Nec Pluribus Impar*: by which they meant, agreeably flattering the ambitions of a young king, that equal in myself to so many things, I would certainly yet be equal to ruling other empires.

In the half-century that lay ahead of him, after Mazarin's death, Louis was to show both the strength and the weakness of his masterful nature. He had persistent energy, and he was devoted to the business of kingship, *le métier de roi*, but his pride and egotism neutralized many of his best qualities. He had no sense of humour and no sense of proportion. At times he believed too firmly in his 'infallibility'. Irrational though it might be, he considered himself to be supremely wise, indeed incapable of human error. He considered himself the source of all renown. 'It seems to me that people take away my glory', so he said, 'when they can acquire it without me.' He was susceptible to flattery, and he became increasingly so with time. He was inclined to assume that the success of ministers and generals was due to his personal inspiration.

Sometimes he was led astray by his creed; but no one could say that he was distracted from public service. His iron constitution, and his insatiable appetite, made him a force of nature which withstood every excess. He devoted nine hours a day to affairs of State. He had an excellent memory and great resourcefulness. Few men could pursue such complex political calculations, or see so many moves ahead. He was patient and untiring, and there is a persistent unity in his policy which was founded on the constant facts in European politics.

The essential characteristic of France during his reign was the fact that it was a government through councils. The councils were largely filled with men of middle-class birth, who owed everything to the King and could not possibly consider themselves to be independent of him. There were four main councils, each of them presided over by the King. The *Conseil d'État*, which consisted of four or five men, met three times a week, to consider the great questions of State; discussion was permitted, but the final decision remained with Louis himself. The *Conseil des Dépêches* considered and decided on all questions that related to home affairs. The *Conseil des Finances* debated questions of taxation. The functions of the *Conseil privé* were deliberately left vague, but it was the highest judicial court in the land, and it represented the undefined but supreme judicial authority that belonged to the Sovereign.

Louis's reign had really begun in 1661, with the death of Mazarin. A few hours after the Cardinal died, he had summoned his first Council. Only three Ministers attended. Michel Le Tellier,

the Secretary for War, was a prudent, conventional administrator. Hugues de Lionne, the acting Secretary for Foreign Affairs, had been the Cardinal's right-hand man for twenty years. Nicolas Fouquet, Attorney-General and Superintendent of Finances, was a wealthy member of the *haute bourgeoisie*. He was forty-five, and brilliantly versatile. He argued philology with the Jesuits, suggested themes to La Fontaine and Corneille, wrote Latin verse, encouraged scientists and collected old masters and rare manuscripts. He had been Superintendent of Finances since 1653. Fouquet expected that the King would let his Council govern the country; his expectations were soon disappointed. Next morning, at a second Council, Louis announced that he would be his own Prime Minister. No one might seal an agreement, sign a despatch or pay a sum of money without his knowledge and command.

Louis began his absolute rule at a nadir in French history. Most of his eighteen million subjects could not understand the French language; they spoke Breton, Languedoc, Flemish or one of many dialects. Most Frenchmen were illiterate, most of them did not have enough to eat. Years of warfare had destroyed houses and farms, and ruined agricultural land. Livestock had been requisitioned and not replaced. The Fronde had bred innumerable lawsuits, and the administration of justice was irregular and corrupt. Theft and murder were amazingly frequent, even in the neighbourhood of Paris. The army lacked discipline, judges and lawyers meddled in the government, absentee bishops neglected their flocks. Industry stagnated, and trade was at a standstill. France was virtually bankrupt.

One of Louis's first measures was to reduce the land tax for 1662 – the heaviest tax on the peasantry – by £1,000,000. He reduced it again in the autumn by a further third of a million. To achieve this, he disbanded a thousand companies of infantry out of a total of eighteen hundred, and six hundred cornets of cavalry out of a thousand. He kept unnecessary expenses to a minimum. No one worked harder for his country than the King himself. Every morning he spent two hours with his inner Council; every afternoon he devoted two or three hours to finances. Every other day he consulted the Chancellor on judicial matters. No pleasure was allowed to interrupt this working day.

None the less, he needed pleasure. Maria Teresa was not beautiful. She had brought from Spain a heavy piety which weighed upon the Court and upon her husband. Louis never entirely neglected her, but he avoided her company, which he found tedious in the

A notable figure in the early years of the reign: Nicolas Fouquet (1615–80), the able and unscrupulous financier who was disgraced by the King in 1661. From the portrait by Bourbon, now at Versailles.

extreme. Maria Teresa took part in all official functions; but, whenever her presence was not required, she led a retired life, more fit for a Carmelite nun than for a queen, and she spent it in good works and in visiting convents.

The most brilliant woman at Court, in the summer of 1661, was Louis's sister-in-law, Madame: Henrietta, the daughter of Charles I and Henrietta-Maria. Henriette – to Gallicize her name – was neglected by her husband, who was a notorious homosexual. She had a roses-and-jasmine complexion, blue eyes and chestnut hair. She sang well and played the spinet, and – which was rare at Court – she had a mind of her own. Louis was delighted by her charm and gaiety.

Anne of Austria saw that he was not in love with his wife. She noticed his affection for Henriette. The Queen Mother was worldly; she recognized that the only way to distract him from Henriette was to interest him in some other lady of the Court. She selected three to tempt him, and among them was Henriette's maid-of-honour, Mlle de La Vallière. In June he first became aware of her.

Louise de La Vallière was seventeen, the daughter of a poor but ardently royalist army officer from Touraine. Mme de Sévigné referred to her as 'that little violet hidden under the grass'; Sainte-Beuve later called her 'a touching rather than triumphant beauty'. A contemporary wrote, more exactly: 'She was not tall, very thin, and walk't with no good Air, because she halted a little; her Complexion very fair, marked with the Small-Pox, her Eyes brown, sometimes languishing and sometimes very fiery and jovial; . . . Constant, Generous, Disinterested, and very Tender and Sincere.' Louis was drawn to her by her simplicity and by her shyness. Almost immediately they fell in love. This time there was no Mazarin to restrain him; and, Bourbon as he was, he longed to love without inhibition. Most people at Court believed that he had no obligation to remain faithful to his official wife. Indeed, it was part of a king's glory to indulge in love-affairs. Had not his grandfather, Henri IV, loved Gabrielle d'Estrées? Louis loved Louise for her sweetness and sincerity; it was clear that she loved him for himself alone. In July 1661 she became his mistress.

He needed personal happiness; for, during the spring and summer, he was engaged in a momentous political battle.

Louis liked clear, analytical minds. On the day after Mazarin's

'Elegant and civilized, a brilliant and subtle diplomat', Cardinal Mazarin. From a portrait by Pierre Mignard.

Three of Mazarin's nieces, Olympe, Hortense and her sister Marie, loved by Louis when he was seventeen. From a painting by an unknown seventeenth-century painter.

Philippe d'Orléans, younger brother of Louis XIV. From a portrait by an unknown artist, now at Versailles.

Henrietta, wife of Philippe d'Orléans and sister of Charles II. After Mignard.

LOVIS·XIV·DANS·SA·MINORITE

OPPOSITE A formal portrait of Louis as a minor. From a painting by Pierre Mignard. LEFT Ceiling of the State Bedroom at Vaux-le-Vicomte. BELOW Louis XIV as a young man. From the portrait by Charles Le Brun.

death, he had appointed Jean-Baptiste Colbert as assistant to Fouquet. Colbert was forty-two and as versatile as Fouquet, but he was endowed with integrity. He soon declared his suspicions of Fouquet's behaviour. The King set Colbert to watch the Superintendent of Finances. Colbert proved conclusively that every afternoon Fouquet was giving the King falsified accounts.

Louis determined to bring Fouquet before a court of law. He saw that he could not order his immediate arrest; first he must get him to resign his post as Attorney-General, otherwise Fouquet could elect to stand trial before his friends in *Parlement*. Louis had learned from Mazarin the art of subtlety. He allowed it to be known that Fouquet could not hold the posts of Chancellor and

Attorney-General at the same time. Fouquet, blind with ambition, fell into the trap, and sold the Attorney-Generalship in the hope of being Chancellor. Dreaming of his dazzling future, he invited the King and Court to his country estate at Vaux-le-Vicomte.

On 17 August, Louis and his entourage arrived at the château. Above the dining-room mantelpiece hung a portrait of the King, painted – without his knowledge – by Le Brun. Fouquet presented it to his sovereign. Two hundred water-spouts and fifty fountains were playing in the gardens; an exquisite meal was served, off gold plate, by Vatel, the Superintendent's *maître-d'hôtel*. In an open-air theatre, Louis watched Molière's farce *Les Fâcheux*; as he returned to the château, thousands of rockets were let off, so that he made his royal progress under a vault of fire.

All this splendour, as Louis knew, was bought with money stolen from the State and, personally, from him. On 5 September, on his orders, Fouquet was arrested. He was tried and sentenced to life-imprisonment in the fortress of Pignerol, in Piedmont. Louis determined to outshine the splendours of Vaux-le-Vicomte by the creation of Versailles. It has been said that he fell in love with Versailles and Louise de La Vallière at the same time; Versailles was the love of his life.

'Constant, Generous, Disinterested, and very Tender and Sincere': Louise de La Vallière, the King's official mistress (1644–1700). From a portrait by J. Nocret.

3 Versailles

VERSAILLES, SOME ELEVEN MILES SOUTH-WEST OF PARIS, had come into royal favour in the previous reign. Louis XIII had built a hunting-lodge near the village to save himself the choice between staying at an inn or riding home to Saint-Germain after a day's sport. It was perhaps as early as 1616 that Louis XIV began to entertain his mistress and his young friends at Versailles; he soon determined to transform the modest hunting-lodge into the very symbol of majesty. He recognized that he must maintain his authority by exploiting the national weakness, vanity, and the dominant national passion for *la gloire*. The palace of Versailles, which he built, is a massive monument to *la gloire*; the Court which he created was devised to flatter vanity. It was the necessary setting for himself, the Sun King, the cynosure of all French eyes. It was a permanent spectacle for the nation.

Louis XIV was not to begin work in earnest at Versailles until 1668; he was to continue alterations and improvements for nearly half a century afterwards. Any survey of Versailles must therefore stretch beyond the chronological point we have reached in his life. But we may well make the survey now, in 1661, at the moment of Fouquet's arrest; for when Fouquet was safely incarcerated at Pignerolles, the King took some of the contents of Vaux – which, after all, had been bought with public money. He then appointed the three remarkable men who had created Vaux, to help him in a project of his own.

Louis Le Vau had been born in 1612. In the Île Saint-Louis, where he lived, he had built the Hôtel Lambert and the Hôtel Lauzun. He was already the architect of the Louvre and the Tuileries when Fouquet had invited him to build the château of Vaux-le-Vicomte (1655-61). Immediately after this, Le Vau was appointed architect of Versailles, and he replanned and enlarged the palace until his death in 1670. He was First Architect to the King, *intendant* and general manager of the royal buildings. He also designed the château of Meudon, the classical buildings and the main courtyard of the Château de Vincennes, the hospital of La Salpêtrière and the plans of the Collège des Quatre Nations, the *Institut de France*.

The second in Louis's remarkable triumvirate was Charles Le Brun (1619-90). He was the son of a master sculptor. In 1642 his protector, the Chancellor Ségnier, had sent him to Rome for three years, and there he had studied the ancient monuments, copied Raphael and consulted his master, Nicolas Poussin. On his return to France he took a decisive part in the establishment of the

PREVIOUS PAGES This equestrian statue of Louis XIV by the great Italian sculptor Bernini failed to earn approval from the King. Converted into a statue of Marcus Curtius by the French sculptor François Girardon, it was relegated to a site near the Eaux des Suisses at Versailles.

OPPOSITE A monument to French classical architecture: Vaux-le-Vicomte, built by Louis Le Vau for Fouquet, 1655–61. This photograph shows the south side of the château.

Académie royale de peinture et de sculpture. The decree of 6 February 1663 made it the academy of the artists who were employed to decorate the royal residences, and Le Brun took control of it. He had in fact already exercised this control as First Painter of the Crown. On 6 March 1663, Louis XIV put him in charge of the Gobelins factory, where the Crown furniture was made. He was to produce not only tapestries, but mosaics, and goldsmiths' and cabinet-makers' work. In spite of his absorbing task, Le Brun found time to make numerous designs for the factory. His facility amazed his contemporaries. It was in fact his responsibility to determine an official style, and this style was fostered by a whole official organization. The practical teaching at the *Académie royale* spread a certain aesthetic conception. In 1666, in order to ensure its unity, Colbert founded an *Académie de France* in Rome; the laureates of the annual academic competition were to go there for three or four years, to finish their education. The *Académie royale* in Paris directed this teaching. Le Brun had laid down its principles: they consisted essentially in correcting the 'imperfections' of nature according to a canon of classical beauty. This doctrine did not prevent Le Brun from painting certain Court portraits with a magisterial assurance. But at Versailles he decorated the Escalier des Ambassadeurs in his classical tradition, and he was also responsible for the Galerie des Glaces, the Salon de la Guerre and the Salon de la Paix.

It is impossible to overestimate the splendour of Versailles: the classical dignity of the architecture and the painting, the baroque opulence of the furniture designed by André-Charles Boulle, glowing with marquetry of copper and tortoiseshell, gleaming with ornaments of carved and gilded bronze. The château of Versailles came to be a monument to *le style Louis XIV*. It ceased to be inhabited at the time of the Revolution, and today it remains an impersonal museum. It also remains the embodiment of the French spirit, the very synthesis of French elegance, a memorial to the most royal of French kings.

Such a palace demanded a handsome setting, and Louis XIV, who had found his architect and his painter, also found his designer of gardens. André Le Nôtre was the son of Jean Le Nôtre, head gardener to Louis XIII, and the grandson of Pierre Le Nôtre, who had been the gardener of the Tuileries in 1592. Born in 1613, Le Nôtre had learned the technical skills of his profession from his family; then he had trained to be an architect, and acquired artistic knowledge in the studios of Simon Vouet and François

Louis. From a pastel by Charles Le Brun.

Mansard. From 1637, he was head gardener at the Tuileries and, in 1638, first gardener at the Luxembourg Gardens. After his marriage in 1640, he was promoted designer of plans (1645), and controller-general of the King's buildings (1656); he received letters of nobility in 1675.

The park of Vaux-le-Vicomte (1651-61) represents the first stage in the evolution of his style, because it is still a composition with a closed perspective. The transformation of the gardens of Versailles and the Tuileries, from 1661, is so extensive that it makes these gardens original works. They mark the second stage in his style, for they create perspectives open on to the infinite. Le Nôtre created his gardens to suit the residence they frame. He also took advantage of the scientific discoveries of his time. He

Two celebrated artists of *le Grand Siècle*: the versatile and influential Charles Le Brun (1619–90) and, *right*, the painter Pierre Mignard (1610–95).

adapted his designs to the laws of optics and hydraulics. Since the discovery of the laws of atmospheric pressure had assured control of water, he added a fairy-tale element to his parks, by introducing fountains like the *grandes eaux* at Versailles. He understood splendour: full-grown forests were transplanted from Normandy and Flanders, nearly fifty thousand bulbs were despatched from Constantinople. Whole regiments were pressed into service to create Versailles, and the Swiss Guards dug the monumental lake which bears their name: a lake which is larger than the Place de la Concorde.

Louis's architects implored him to pull down his father's hunting-lodge because it made their work so difficult. He answered that if, for some reason, the lodge disappeared, he would recon-

Patron of the arts: Louis XIV (left of centre, wearing hat) is seen at the Gobelins tapestry works with Colbert.

Monsieur Roy de Perse

struct it brick by brick. His courtiers protested – as far as they dared to protest – that there was no view. Saint-Simon considered Versailles to be 'the saddest and most barren of places, with no view, no wood, no water, and no earth, for it is all shifting sand and marsh, and the air, in consequence, is bad'. Mme de Sévigné wrote of 'the great mortality afflicting the workmen, of whom every night wagons full of the dead are carried out as though from the Hôtel-Dieu. These melancholy processions are kept secret as far as possible, in order not to alarm the other workmen.' Primi Visconti, an Italian observer, added later in the century: 'The air is foul there. In addition, the putrid waters infest the air so vilely that during the month of August everyone fell ill. . . . Yet the King insists on living there.'

Louis brushed aside any criticism of Versailles. The high mortality rate among the workmen meant nothing to their sovereign; and if he had deigned to answer those who wanted a grander prospect, he would have said that he loved the typical view of the Île de France. He was a country person, and Versailles had some special charm for him. He had no intention of living in Paris, as Colbert was anxious for him to do; and he had no intention of reducing the colossal expenses of his new palace. And so the work on Versailles continued, and he constantly paid visits to the site to see how the work was progressing. On 17 February 1663, M Petit, Colbert's steward, reported to his employer:

My Lord, immediately the King arrived at Versailles yesterday, he enquired what new work had been done since the previous occasion His Majesty had been there and whether the works were making progress. We told him that the frost was preventing us from finishing the plastering of the interior of the main buildings and pavilion of the kitchen and stables, . . . but that all these surfaces were lathed and could be finished in three weeks of good weather and that His Majesty should receive satisfaction from our diligence then. . . .

Our labourers, eighty in number, are working as I described to you in my letter. I am assured that a fresh team is due to arrive on Monday and these I shall put to work immediately. Three hundred and fifty labourers are working mightily at shifting the earth for the Orangerie and the semi-lune from the end of the *grand parterre*. . . .

More than twenty years later, on 27 August 1684, the Marquis de Dangeau recorded: 'During this last week, the sum of 250,000 livres has been spent on Versailles. Every day 22,000 men and 6,000 horses were working there.'

At first the King did more work on the gardens than on the

Monsieur in fancy dress as the King of Persia at a carousel seen by ten thousand spectators.

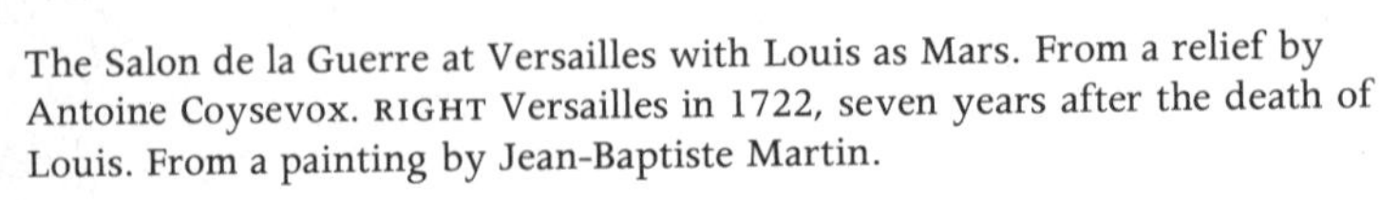

The Salon de la Guerre at Versailles with Louis as Mars. From a relief by Antoine Coysevox. RIGHT Versailles in 1722, seven years after the death of Louis. From a painting by Jean-Baptiste Martin.

The Gardens of Versailles

If Versailles is the lasting symbol of the best and most splendid aspect of Louis, the choice of its site shows a mixture of perversity and arrogance. From the beauties of France, Louis selected a featureless hunting ground and where God had contrived only a marsh, Louis laid out the most impressive gardens in Europe. As there was no view, he created one.

BELOW The Marly Machine: an early experiment in hydraulics, designed to bring the waters of the Seine to the royal château.
BELOW RIGHT Grand, inhuman and theatrical, the gardens at Versailles reflect the style of Louis XIV.

LEFT André Le Nôtre (1613–1700). Controller-general of the King's buildings, he transformed the gardens at Versailles and at the Tuileries.
RIGHT La Fontaine de Flore: one of the elaborate ornaments of the gardens at Versailles. The King is seen on horseback on the left. From an engraving by Lepautre.

palace, following the lines laid down by Louis XIII. He added more and more 'green rooms', which he used for ever more elaborate parties. In 1664 he gave a fête called *Les Plaisirs de l'Île Enchantée,* which lasted from 7-13 May.

The King, wishing to give the Queens and all his Court the pleasure of some unusual Festivities, in a place adorned with all the delights that can make a Country House admired, chose Versailles, four leagues from Paris. It is a Château which might be called an enchanted Palace, so well have the arrangements of art enhanced the care that Nature has taken to make it perfect. It charms in every way. Everything is smiling there, without and within. Gold and marble vie in beauty and in brilliance. . . . Its Symmetry, the richness of its furnishings, the beauty of its walks, & the infinite number of its flowers and of its orange-trees, make the surroundings of this place worthy of its singular rarity. . . .

It was in this setting that the fêtes were held. Noblemen, clad as knights, competed in an arena in the *course de bague*: catching rings off a pole with their lances, as they galloped past. At nightfall on the first day, so a chronicler observed,

the arena was lit by countless flambeaux, and, the knights having retired, there appeared the Orpheus of our days – I am referring, of course, to Lully – at the head of a great company of performers who, after approaching the Queens in short steps in time to their instruments, divided into two columns passing on each side of the high dais and proceeding alongside the palisades bordering the *rond.* At the same time, there emerged from the avenue on the right-hand side the Four Seasons: Spring on a great Spanish horse, Summer on an elephant, Autumn on a camel and Winter on a bear. The Seasons were accompanied by twelve gardeners, twelve reapers, twelve wine-harvesters, and twelve old men. They indicated the difference between their Seasons by flowers, wheatsheafs, fruits and mirrors, and carried on their heads great bowls in which were heaped the ingredients of the collation which was to follow.

During the week-long festival, the King himself performed in a ballet. According to the official account, he was

mounted on one of the finest horses in the world, whose flame-coloured harness glittered with gold and silver and precious stones. His Majesty was armed in the fashion of the Greeks, like everyone else in his Quadrille, & he wore a cuirass of silver plate, covered with a rich embroidery of gold & of diamonds. His bearing & his whole behaviour were worthy of his rank: his Helmet, all covered with flame-coloured plumes, had an incomparable grace.

In 1665 Bernini paid his visit to France – the only visit he would make abroad. Architect, sculptor and painter, he was the founder of the monumental and decorative baroque. His versatility, fire and audacity imposed him on his contemporaries. He seems like the stage-manager of an epoch. Now, yielding to the demands of Louis XIV and Colbert, he arrived from Rome to design the main façade of the Louvre. The King rejected his plans, and it was then that the classical doctrine triumphed at Court; from this point of view, Bernini's journey marks an epoch in the history of French art. Before he went home, he had also sculpted his brilliant and convincing bust of the King; it was in Rome that he sculpted the equestrian statue of Louis XIV. This masterpiece did not please the King, and it was relegated to the place which it has kept ever since: on the edge of the *Eau des Suisses*, a long way from the palace.

In 1668, when the King set to work in earnest on Versailles, he gave a *Divertissement* there to mark the occasion. During the evening, Molière produced his comedy *Georges Dandin* for the first time. Three hundred women were invited to the royal supper. Louise de La Vallière sat next to the King, but – so we are told – he constantly looked at another table where the Marquise de Montespan and her friend Mme Scarron were keeping the guests in delighted laughter. Years later, people remembered the evening which had contained the past, the present and the future.

A few days after the *Divertissement*, the 'envelope' of Versailles was begun. The King had decided, with the help of Le Vau, to envelop his father's hunting-lodge in his own palace. He also turned his attention to the new town of Versailles. It was laid out by Le Nôtre, and land was given to people who undertook to build houses to an approved specification.

Louis's prestige and the fame of Versailles increased every year. Generations of workmen laboured on, for he was perpetually making alterations and improvements. Voltaire later described Versailles as a great *caravanserai* filled with human discomfort and misery; but the misery was not generally visible, and the grandeur was clear to all.

The background of the monarchy remained Versailles, and in 1682 the residence of the Court was fixed there. The Court was the ornamental framework of monarchy; it was also a brilliant political game. The high nobility flocked to Versailles; and, far from their sources of strength in the provinces, they devoted themselves to palace intrigues, while their ladies disputed the right to sit on a

FOLLOWING PAGES Louis XIV inspects the Gobelins factory, which contributed so much to the official art of his reign. His visit is commemorated in a tapestry of astonishing opulence.

Les Plaisirs de l'Ile Enchantée: a scene on the first day of the festivities held at Versailles in May 1664. The King is seen (centre, front) escorted by his knights; Apollo is seated on the triumphal chariot.

FOLLOWING PAGES The château of Versailles: a massive monument to the dominant French passion for *la gloire*.

miere Journée.
de la feste, faite par les recits d'Apollon et des quatre
siecles, assis sur vn grand Char de triomphe.
3

small stool in the Queen's presence. There was an unremitting struggle for the sinecures and pensions which consoled the *noblesse* for their loss of power. By destroying their political power, and leaving them their privileges, Louis XIV was preparing the way for the Revolution. But the Sun King wanted the meanest detail to assume importance beneath his rays. Such were the nuances of etiquette, so we are told, that he had forty different ways of doffing his hat, according to the person whom he was greeting. In order to distinguish his principal courtiers, he devised blue cloaks embroidered in gold and silver; the privilege of wearing them was considered a high favour, and they were almost as much in demand as the collar of the Order of Saint-Louis.

Versailles was now not only a palace; it was also a town and the centre of the administration. The palace alone accommodated ten thousand people, and in its vicinity there were fifty thousand more. Versailles was a world – a totally artificial world – of its own. Most of the day was spent in the solemn and regular manner which Louis had laid down when Mazarin died. 'With an almanach and a watch,' said Saint-Simon, 'one can say what he is doing three hundred leagues away.'

And so one could. At seven o'clock every morning, the first valet of the bedchamber slipped out of the King's room, in which he had been sleeping. He dressed in the ante-chamber, and returned fifteen minutes later. A servant lit a fire in the fireplace. In the meanwhile, other servants opened the shutters, and removed the silver lamp and candle and the first valet's bedding. The first valet approached the King's bed and pronounced the ritual words: 'Sire, it is time.' Then he opened the door.

Even before the *grandes entrées*, the formal admission of the first courtiers, the first physician and the first surgeon had entered through the back door of the chamber. With them was Perette Dufour, a carter's wife from Poissy. The former wet-nurse to the King, she came every day until her death in 1688 to kiss him good-morning, while the others rubbed him down and changed his nightshirt.

Then came the *grandes entrées*.

Those who had entry and might see the King while he was still in bed were Monseigneur [the Dauphin]; the dukes of Burgundy, Berri, Orléans and Bourbon; the Duc dú Maine and the Comte de Toulouse. These were members of the royal family. Similarly privileged by virtue of their office were the grand chamberlain, the four first gentlemen of the bedchamber, the grand master and masters of the robes, the four first valets

of the chamber and the first valet of the wardrobe on duty, the first physician and the first surgeon (who were already present), and all who had held these offices in the past or who enjoyed the reversion of them.

Saint-Simon said that the *grandes entrées* were 'the mark of rare and signal favour, and deprivation of them was the greatest and most useful punishment'.

The grand chamberlain or the first gentleman of the bedchamber drew aside the bed curtains. While the King was still in bed, the first valet poured spirits of wine over His Majesty's hands. The holy water font was presented to the King, who dipped his hand and made the sign of the Cross. The person who had presented the holy water then presented the prayer book with the office of the Holy Ghost and all retired to the council chamber, while the King remained in prayer. Fifteen minutes later, he recalled them to his room. Then the royal barber, Quentin, appeared, bringing two or more wigs of different lengths (the King began to wear a wig in 1672). The King chose his wig, and rose from his bed, slipping his feet into mules which were offered to him by the first valet. Then the grand chamberlain wrapped His Majesty in his dressing-gown.

Louis XIV then seated himself in an armchair by the fire, to hold what was called his *petit lever*. The grand chamberlain had removed the King's nightcap, and one of the barbers was combing his hair, for, even when he wore a wig, the King did not always have his own hair shaven. Now the *secondes entrées* began. They were accorded to four secretaries of the dressing-room, the first valets of the wardrobe off duty, the two lectors of the chamber, the two major-domos and wardens of the plate, and those who enjoyed the reversion of these offices or had occupied them in the past. They were also accorded to the chief apothecary, and to the physician and surgeon on duty.

When the King's hair had been combed, he put on the periwig for his *lever*; this was shorter than the one he would wear for the rest of the day. As the officers of the robes approached to dress him, he called for the ushers of his bedchamber. They took their places at the door and admitted the valets, the cloak bearers, the arquebus bearers and other officers of the chamber.

This was the moment when cardinals, archbishops, dukes and generals, and other people of quality, were allowed an audience of the King. While the audience was being held, the royal *toilette* continued. Louis was given his breeches with silk stockings

PREVIOUS PAGES An allegorical portrait of the royal family. From left to right: Queen Henrietta Maria of England as Amphytrite, the Queen of the Sea; her son-in-law, Philippe (Monsieur) as Pluto; his wife, Henrietta-Anne as Flora, with their daughter Marie-Louise between them; Anne of Austria, Louis's mother, suitably as Cybele, mother of the gods; Mlle d'Orléans, a cousin, as one of the Graces; Louis as Apollo; his wife Maria Teresa as Juno, touching the hand of the Dauphin; and Mlle de Montpensier, another cousin, as Diana. The cherubim are unidentified Bourbon off-spring, with the two framed children probably Anne Elizabeth and Marie Anne who died as infants. From a painting by an unknown artist, circa 1670.

attached, and his pumps, which usually had diamond buckles. When he asked for his breakfast, he was brought two cups of sage and angelica tea, but he was not allowed to drink them until the formalities of tasting had been completed. Originally he had taken a bit of bread with wine and water. He never drank tea or chocolate. After breakfast, the Dauphin (or, in his absence, the Duc de Berri or the Duc d'Orléans) handed the King a shirt faced with white taffeta. The valets of the wardrobe brought the sword, the jacket and the *Cordon Bleu* – the Order of the Saint-Esprit. When he was dressed, the King said a prayer, then he went into his dressing-room and put on his ordinary wig. He was followed into the room by those whose offices entitled them to do so; he gave each of them the orders of the day.

At ten o'clock, His Majesty was in the Grande Galerie; he passed through all the rooms of his apartments before he reached the chapel. On his return from Mass, he summoned his council. By one o'clock he was ready to dine. Saint-Simon recorded that 'he ate so prodigiously and so substantially morning and evening that no-one could grow accustomed to witnessing it'. One member of his family confessed: 'I have often seen the King consume four full plates of different kinds of soup, an entire pheasant, a partridge, a large dish of salad, two large slices of ham, mutton with gravy and garlic, a whole tray of pastries, and then fruit and hard-boiled eggs.' Until 1694 dinner was washed down with champagne, but after that year old burgundies were served.

Saint-Simon described the ceremony of dinner in some detail:

> In the morning the King ordered a simple, or very simple, meal, but even the latter consisted of three courses, not to mention the fruit and numerous dishes. When the table had been set, the principal courtiers entered (they themselves had dined earlier, at noon), followed by all who were recognized at Court. . . .
>
> I have seen Monsieur [the King's brother] there quite often. . . . He would serve the napkin (moistened at one end, dry at the other, so that the King might wash and dry his hands) between two vermeil plates and would then hesitate for a moment. The King, seeing that he did not withdraw, would ask if he might not wish to be seated. He bowed, and the King ordered a chair to be brought; a tabouret would be placed behind him. A few moments later the King would say: 'Be seated, *mon frère*.' Monsieur would bow and sit down until the end of the dinner, when he would again serve the napkin. . . .

When Louis XIV had a grand public dinner, there was even more

Louis XIV playing billiards. Even when he followed such innocuous pursuits, he wore his plumed hat as a status-symbol.

elaborate ceremony. An ordinance of 1681 set down the procedure for serving the meat that was ready in the pantry:

The gentleman who is serving carries the first dish; the second is carried by the warden; the officers of the pantry bring the others. In this order they advance in procession towards the table, with the major-domo at their head carrying his staff in his hand. The usher of the table, carrying a stick – and in the evening a torch – marches a few paces ahead of them. When the meat arrives accompanied by three bodyguards with muskets on their shoulders, the major-domo bows to the *nef* (the hexagonal salver on which are arranged the King's plate and cutlery). The gentleman who is serving places his dish on the table, next to the *nef*.

The afternoons were spent on hunting and shooting expeditions (the King sometimes bagged sixty birds in the space of two or three hours). Sometimes there were outings and picnics with the ladies of the Court. At the end of the day came the *appartement*, the gathering of the whole Court. This took place every Monday, Wednesday and Friday from October to Palm Sunday, 'between seven and ten o'clock, when the King sat down to table'. The *appartement* was held in the state apartments stretching across the garden side of Versailles, from the vestibule of the Chapel to the Hall of Mirrors. Surrounded by gold and marble, green or flame-coloured velvet, illumined by a myriad candles, the Court

Pomp and circumstance at the Court of the Sun King: Louis XIV receives the Siamese Ambassadors in 'royal and magnificent audience'.

FOLLOWING PAGES The building of Versailles. From a painting by Van der Meulen. By Gracious Permission of H.M. the Queen.

listened to music, danced, played cards and billiards, drank wine and 'all sorts of fruit drinks'. Louis, escorted only by the captain of the guard, strolled graciously among his guests.

The King spent his life in public from birth to death; and, it is said, he would as soon have neglected his council as his *grand couvert*, at which he dined in the presence of his subjects. He forced himself to the ceremony less than a week before he died. He himself was never bored by the ritual he had established, because he knew the reason for it. Some of those who had to take part found it unbearable. Mme de Maintenon wrote to her brother: 'I know of no one more unfortunate than the highest in the land, except for the people who envy them.' One day, as she looked at the famous carps in the lake at Fontainebleau, she said: 'They are like me, they regret their mind.'

Such comments were far from ridiculous. Life at Court was always harassing. Receptions, festivities and military reviews continued without interruption, and with the strictest observance of etiquette. Wherever the King went, he exacted a service that amounted to slavery. The organization of his household presented a striking contrast between the splendour of his royal state and the discomfort of his domestic arrangements. The inmates of Versailles burned tallow candles and put their legs into bags filled with straw to keep themselves warm. Only royalty had wax candles, and enough wood to keep fires alight. The sanitary arrangements baffled description – and this was not surprising, for there was no water. However, an attempt was made to carry the waters of the Eure from Maintenon to Versailles by an aqueduct which was to rival those of ancient Rome. Between 1684 and 1688 a whole army of workmen, most of them soldiers, were busy building it. The country was so marshy and unhealthy that thousands of them died of fever. 187,000,000 francs were squandered on the undertaking, which finally had to be abandoned as impracticable. Versailles cost 400,000,000 francs to build, and it estranged the King from the nation. This moral loss was far more serious than the material damage done by the King's insane prodigality.

In the isolation of Versailles, Louis never came into contact with the forces which were shaping the minds of a new generation. He lived far away from the capital. Paris and his *Parlement* no longer saw him. He did not recognize that a spirit of independence and growing opposition was rising up against the system which he represented. As long as he was successful, these signs of discontent were hardly noticeable, even to experienced observers, but they were growing.

Louis did not devote himself only to Versailles. In his youth he had been fond of Fontainebleau, and even after the creation of Versailles, the Court went to Fontainebleau once a year. Between 1679 and 1690 Louis spent a great deal of money on the palace of Marly, to which he became much attached in later life; and he used to arrive there on Wednesday, leaving again on Saturday in order to spend Sunday at Versailles. There was, of course, much competition at Court to accompany him to Marly: *être des Marly*, as it was termed. Such was the unreal world in which Louis moved. La Bruyère wrote of the Court, with truth:

> It is a country in which the joys are visible but false, and the sorrows are hidden but real. Who would believe that the enthusiasm for entertainments, the applause at the brilliant plays of Molière and the Harlequinades, the feasts, the hunting parties, ballets and tournaments conceal so much disquiet, so many cares and conflicting interests, so many hopes and fears, such lively passions and such serious matters?

4

The State of the Nation

THE KING KNEW LITTLE ABOUT LIFE IN PARIS, for he seldom went there. However, during his reign there arose a number of buildings and architectural features which were worthy of *le Grand Siècle*. Among them were the Observatory, the Gobelins factory, the colonnade of the Louvre, the dome of the Invalides, the Porte Saint-Martin and the Porte Saint-Denis, the Place Vendôme and the Place des Victoires. At the same time the Champs-Élysées were developed, and the Tuileries completed, while the simple but superb Pont-Royal replaced a wooden structure over the Seine. Most of this achievement must be attributed to bourgeois officials, and in particular to Colbert. It was Colbert who argued that Paris should not extend beyond certain limits. Indeed the reign of Louis XIV shows the first intelligent modern planning in the capital.

Jean-Baptiste Colbert was a brilliant adviser in a brilliant age. Born in 1619, he had started his career at the Ministry of War under Le Tellier, but he had first made his mark as assistant to Mazarin, who had recommended him to the King. When Colbert had helped to overthrow Fouquet, he took his place as *intendant des finances*. In 1665 he became *contrôleur-général*. He determined to turn France into a hive of activity, to promote and direct French industries, to protect them from foreign rivalry by high protective tariffs and then to open up trade. He pursued this task with energy, and with as much success as his commercial theory, the tepid interest of the King and the state of the country allowed.

The first step was to make France prosperous and independent. Colbert devised a sound administrative organization. The royal bureaucracy took over the government of the country. France was divided into *généralités* under royal *intendants*. These functionaries were sent out by the royal council, and in due course they returned to it. Through their correspondence the life of France passed before the council, which – in its different divisions – sat every day. In 1667 the Paris police were organized under their first Lieutenant, Nicolas-Gabriel de La Reynie. For thirty years La Reynie worked to make the capital safer, cleaner and healthier. The streets were lit by five thousand lamps, and the number of police was quadrupled.

Such measures were not always taken to satisfy the people. Louis XIV lived intoxicated by the idea of his own greatness and invincible power. The thought of any opposition was intolerable, neither public nor private criticism was allowed; the police became the chief bulwark of the government. The centralized

PREVIOUS PAGES 'The Academy of Sciences and the Fine Arts dedicated to the King.' A symbolic engraving by Sebastien Le Clerc.

OPPOSITE Jean-Baptiste Colbert (1619–83), the great finance minister of Louis XIV. Colbert, who was also minister of marine, created a powerful French navy; he founded several academies, collected pictures and statues for the Louvre, and extended and reorganized the royal library. A patron of scholarship, he was without question one of the most versatile, gifted and influential men of the reign. This portrait of him, now at Versailles, was painted by Lefebvre.

One of the architectural monuments to *le Grand Siècle*: the dome of the Invalides, built by Jules Hardouin-Mansard.

system designed by Richelieu and Mazarin was carried, now, to its logical conclusion. The States-General were never summoned. Louis set out to destroy the provincial differences of France, and to impose a uniform administration over the whole country. Municipal liberties were destroyed on the pretext of bad financial administration. The King's *intendants* were supported and strengthened against all opposition.

Despite the centralizing policy of Richelieu, Colbert and Louis XIV, total unity was never attained in France. Many anomalies and local customs still survived from an earlier age. In administration, law and commerce, France remained divided within itself. When the Revolution finally destroyed these anomalies, it produced a reorganized France which was more centralized than ever.

A study of the administration shows that there was a difference between the *pays d'élection* and the *pays d'états*. The *pays d'élection* were areas in which the royal taxes were assessed and levied by Crown officials. The *pays d'états*, however, had their own provincial *parlements*, which noted and assessed the money demanded by the Crown. These Estates also controlled local works and industry, and they often showed vigorous feeling, determined independence. The Bretons had their own constitution and declared that, if they were French, it was only because the King also happened to be the Duc de Bretagne. The men of Provence and the Dauphiné asserted a similar independence. The royal *intendants* did much to diminish the importance of local *parlements*, but the provinces still kept their local institutions and no *intendant* could afford to disregard their wishes.

In law there were differences, too. France was divided into two main legal areas. The south was the land of 'written' law, or *droit écrit*, where Roman Law, modified by local usage, was the rule. The centre and north was the land of 'customary' law, or *droit coutumier*; and countless different feudal customs, like the *coutume de Paris*, were observed here. There was, of course, great variety in both areas – but especially in the north.

Even where commerce was concerned, France was not unified. The people of Languedoc had long exchanged their goods freely with Spain, and they resisted royal interference with this arrangement. In 1642, Louis XIII had found himself obliged to set up customs houses between Languedoc and the rest of France. In 1664, Colbert tried to remove all local dues, and to establish a uniform duty along the frontier. But local resistance was so strong that he succeeded in bringing some uniformity to only fourteen northern provinces. There were, one might add, two other kinds of customs area in France. The southern provinces kept their tariffs, and any wares passing to and fro from the rest of the kingdom were subject to duty. Moreover, the eastern provinces were not part of France at all, economically speaking; they were outside the national customs frontier, and they made their own tariff arrangements with other countries.

Colbert was not only a great finance minister, administrator and economic reformer. He was also given charge of the colonies and the navy. In 1664 he set up an enquiry to determine the number and quality of the vessels in French ports. There were only 2,368 vessels over ten tons. The greatest and most lasting of Colbert's achievements was the re-establishment of the French navy. It has been said that in 1661, when he took office, there were only thirty armed ships in France, of which only three had more than sixty guns. When he died, in 1683, there were 107 ships with from 24 to 120 guns, not to mention many smaller vessels. For the maintenance and use of this navy, Colbert reconstructed the works and arsenal of Toulon, founded the port and arsenal of Rochefort, and the naval schools of Rochefort, Dieppe and St Malo; and he fortified, among other ports, Calais, Dunkirk, Brest and Le Havre. Determined to attract recruits to his growing navy, he invented his famous *inscription maritime*, which is still in use. This divided all seamen into classes; each seaman, according to his class, gave six months' service every three, four or five years. For three months after his term of service, a sailor was placed on half-pay; pensions were promised. Colbert also founded prizes for naval construction. Everything was done to make the navy popular. Nor was the merchant navy forgotten. Shipbuilding was encouraged by allowing a premium on ships bought at home, and by imposing a duty on those bought from abroad.

These naval and maritime developments allowed wide economic enterprise. Colbert decided to form two great trading companies, one for the East Indies and the other for the West. In 1664 he obtained his edicts, which virtually divided the world into two and gave half to each company to exploit. Colbert established further companies which had interests in very diverse fields. Meanwhile, a sound economic foundation was being laid at home. Factories were created. It was Colbert who reorganized the old cloth industry in Languedoc so that it could compete successfully in the markets of the Levant. French workmen were prohibited from emigrating, and foreign workmen were encouraged to settle in France. Venetian glassmakers, coppersmiths from Liège, German miners and Scandinavian pitch-burners were all settled in France to boost French productivity. This policy had considerable success. It was a healthy sign that, at the end of the century, many firms were to ask that full competitive trading should be restored. Then, between 1697 and 1713, the French government signed commercial treaties with England, Holland, Prussia, Denmark and the Hanseatic ports. Under Colbert, also, communications were improved. It was Colbert who sponsored the great project of a canal between the Atlantic and the Mediterranean. This was completed in 1681.

Colbert's achievement was not so great as it might have been. He needed peace to carry out his programme of economic and naval expansion; but the war department was in the hands of his rival Louvois, whose influence with the King gradually supplanted his own. Louvois encouraged all the King's aggressive instincts; and Louis did not need much encouragement to go to war. France therefore spent its resources in a series of continental wars which continued nearly fifty years, at the cost of its commerce and its colonies. When Lous XIV died in 1715, he left his kingdom bankrupt and distressed. Its state contrasted strongly with the prosperous state of England.

Posterity, however, remains amazed at the variety of subjects to which Colbert gave his attention, and at the diligence which he displayed. No French statesman was to be so versatile and energetic until Napoleon, more than a century later. Colbert worked harder than anyone in France. He used to enter his study at half past five in the morning and he spent up to sixteen hours a day at his desk. He could be a harsh master. A merchant who had failed to produce enough tin was informed that His Majesty's needs must be met with prompt and adequate supplies. Colbert could also be a self-seeking overlord. He provided well for his family during his years in power, and he amassed a huge fortune for himself. But Louis XIV owed him much of his glory. Colbert collected pictures and statues for the Louvre; he extended and reorganized the royal library, and he formed a great library of his own. He was the active patron of men of learning. The creation of five new Academies was due to Colbert: the Academy of Inscriptions and Medals, the French Academy at Rome, the Academy of Architecture, the Academy of Music and the Academy of Science. One of the conditions of membership of the Academy of Science, founded in 1666, decreed that those admitted should

A merchant banker at work in the days of Louis XIV. A contemporary engraving.

communicate to fellow-members the results of their enquiries. Science benefited by Colbert's initiative, and by Louis's patronage. Thanks to new facilities at the Observatory in Paris, Cassini discovered four satellites round Saturn, which he respectfully called Ludovici, and Roemer calculated the speed of light from the satellites of Jupiter. In 1699 Louis enlarged the Academy of Science.

Colbert took an active interest in the public works of Paris, and he hoped – though in vain – to make the King concentrate his

AMI IUSQU'A LA BOURSE.
Tel Expose gayement
Sa vie pour son amy
Qui ne luy preteroit
pas une pistole
Sans chagrin
L'un ne prete pas Volontiers et lautre rend le plus tard qu'il peut
Se vend a paris chez Guerard Graveur rue St Jacques a la reyne du clerge proche S yues. C P R

architectural ambitions on the Louvre. He protested against the expense of Versailles with remarkable frankness.

As a bourgeois, he also considered that control was essential to everyday life. It suited his schemes that the working man should be subjected to rules, and that guilds and statutes should regulate his movements. And here, perhaps, we may turn for a moment to the bourgeoisie and the labouring classes: to the less familiar and less glamorous side of *le Grand Siècle.*

As far as the common people were concerned, the change in the balance of power between the social orders in France brought little respite from their eternal miseries. But other classes of society were much better off under Louis XIV than they were under faction and disorder: these were the middle classes, from which Louis chose his principal Ministers and advisers. The centre of gravity had shifted from Paris to Versailles, the noble had become a mere palace servant, but the Third Estate in the towns was flourishing.

Despite their new-found freedoms, merchants and businessmen found one aspect of commerce frustrating. The second half of the century was a time of deflation. There was not enough currency to meet the needs of a growing economy. Prices therefore tended to fall, and taxes could not be collected in full. The gold mines of Colombia, Peru and Mexico were still producing quantities of gold, but there was not enough to go round. The States of Languedoc could not float a loan because there was not enough money in circulation.

Shortage of money also had an adverse effect on agriculture; the farmers of Provence could not sell some of their corn to other provinces, because the other provinces could not pay for it. When it was announced at Bordeaux that some of the specie in stock was to be transferred to Paris, there was a panic. Mme de Sévigné complained in many of her letters that she was short of money, and that economic reasons obliged her to retire to her country house, so that she might live on the produce of her own farm. A person in the second half of the century, said Mme de Sévigné, could count on only a quarter of his revenues. Lack of money dried up commerce and prevented sales. Prices dropped by a third in the half century, and people tended to wait and save and to do nothing.

Industrial finance remained the biggest problem. The money that had to be paid out to creditors of the State was a great

Lender and borrower.
An engraving of the period.

obstacle to industrialization. Colbert could not accept the idea that people should live on unearned income, and he detested the sale of sinecures to bourgeois who aspired to the ranks of the nobility. Yet the King tended to create more and more useless State offices which his subjects might purchase; and traffic in State offices was so lucrative that in wartime even Colbert had to accept a distasteful necessity – the necessity of the money-lender, like Samuel Bernard, for example, who could virtually have his own way with the King.

Yet, in spite of economic stresses, the middle classes seem to have lived contentedly under Louis XIV. They led a life of comparative ease, surrounded by the rewards of industry and careful investment. Their furniture was made of the finest wood and it looked as if it were made to last for ever. Their houses became larger and larger.

Middle-class children received the education their parents could afford, which meant that many boys had private tutors, while girls still tended to go to convent schools, where the emphasis was on religious instruction. After their private tuition, the boys were usually sent to college. The colleges taught religion, but, thanks partly to the paganism of the classical authors they prescribed, they managed to turn out a number of free-thinkers. *Mariages de convenance* remained the rule and not the exception.

Yet, old-fashioned though they might be in some ways, the middle classes were still none the less concerned with keeping up with current trends and vogues. This sometimes led to conflict with authority, for the King – still determined to be exalted above all his subjects – even tried to regulate fashion. For example, a decree of 1660 renewed an earlier edict of 1656 forbidding the middle-classes to wear clothe-of-gold or -silver. Even though the decree expressed the royal preference, it had to be re-issued eleven times: a fact which shows how wealthy (and how independent) the middle classes were.

The fashions of the day were presented to the public through the columns of the *Mercure galant*, and every bourgeois attempted, of course, to imitate Versailles. The most striking feature of male attire was the profusion of ribbons attached to the shoulder, the sleeve and the garter; ruffs called canons adorned each leg between the calf and thigh. As for wigs, a man could choose the perruque *à la royale, in folio, à la brigadière, à la robin* or *à la moutonne bouclée*. After 1703 wigs were powdered, and every year there were slight variations in fashion. Some wigs were so

Mariage à la mode. The prospective wife is accepted, since her financial advantages compensate for her personal failings.

ARGENT FAIT TOUT
Pour marier un Enfant richement deux ou trois sont mis au Couvent
N'arque à l'amour et vive la marmite
On pèze l'or et non pas le merite
Suplement aux deffauts personels

PEINTURE SANS MAITRISE.
Laissons gloser ces esprits mal timbrés
Par un bel Art reparons la nature
Cachons sous la couleur, nos attraits delabrés
Et nous aurons un teint fleuri en mignature
Un teint bien refait et d'un éclat merveilleux
Oui Madame je voit désja briller vos Yeux
L'admirable Art que la Peinture
C'est un tresor, qu'enrichit la nature
Car je voit qu'a chaque coup de pinceau
Vôtre teint prend un éclat tout nouveau
Sur tout quand vous jouez de la prunelle
O Ciel que d'Esclaves en vous voyant si belle
En vous voyant on voit la mere des Amours
Qui triomphe des cœurs mais plaçons en vedette
Prés de l'oeil l'assasin et la mouche coquette
Et nous verrons tantost beau jeu au cours.
Peignes de Plomb servant a peindre les cheveux roux en brun
Methode de peindre en mignature sur le cuir et la peau.
la Fille écoute et voit elle sa mere, jour ce voit faire
aprend de a faire un quelle luy
Arsenal de la mollesse
Artillerie des Coquettes
Iris croit par le fard d'étre belle et de plaire
Son visage plâtré n'est qu'un mauvais ragoust
Elle gâte son teint en croyant le refaire
Et pretend plaire en donnant du degoust.
LA TOILLETTE

enormous that it became the habit to carry the hat under the arm.

Women's hair-styles began to evolve in 1671, when Mme Martin launched the *hurluberlu* style; this meant cutting off quite a quantity of hair. In 1680 Mlle de Fontanges started another vogue by sweeping her hair up into a turban. The resulting fashion, *une coiffure à la Fontanges*, lasted for twenty years. Beauty spots were all the rage under Louis XIV, and they spoke a symbolic language of their own. The *passionnée*, for example, was set near the eye, while the *coquette* was close to the lips and the *galante* on the cheek. The *effrontée* appeared on the nose.

Considering this outward show of elegance, it is strange that so little attention was paid to the body itself. There were no such things as bathrooms in private *hôtels*, but if the bather felt uninclined to travel to the bath-house, he could hire a portable *baignoire* for the day. Water was still considered slightly dangerous, and one newspaper warned its readers that 'washing in water is bad for the sight, it produces toothache and catarrh. It also makes the complexion pale, exposing the face to cold in winter and to sunburn in summer.' However, though there was a general distaste for water and for washing, it was fashionable at Versailles to attend the royal bathing-parties. The custom spread to Paris, and bathing establishments by the Seine began to attract clientele. Ladies were expected to bathe in the comparative seclusion of bath-houses anchored in the river. In 1675 we learn that men who aspired to cleanliness were being urged to wash their feet regularly, and that Turkish baths were flourishing. A manual of gallantry explained to its readers: 'One may sometimes go to the bath-house in order to have a clean body, and everyday one should take the trouble to wash one's hands with milk of almonds. The face must be washed almost as often.'

Cleanliness and hygiene did not unduly concern the bourgeois in the reign of Louis XIV. It need hardly be said that food remained a paramount interest. The *Cuisinier de Varenne*, a contemporary recipe-book, offered a selection of twenty-three *potages, entrées, entremets, sauces* and *pâtés*. Seasoning was much in fashion (due partly, no doubt, to the difficulties of preserving meat and poultry); and some dishes were flavoured with rose-water. In ordinary houses, large quantities of beans and lentils were consumed. Asparagus and sorrel were generally preferred to cabbage and potatoes, but artichokes were plentiful. The subjects of *le Roi Soleil* were – like Queen Anne – much addicted to green peas. Since peas were seasonal, they were a luxury, and in 1660 the

Fashions and cosmetics are gently mocked in this engraving of the period.

King received some from Italy packed in herbs and roses. Fish was not often eaten, largely because of transport problems. Oysters were favoured, eaten raw or grilled in their shells, and sardines with wine were a great delicacy. Fruit was abundant. It was the custom to peel the fruit and replace it in its skin before it was served. In about 1648 there was a revolution in table manners, when the plate replaced a slice of bread as a receptacle for food; in about 1655 there was another revolution in manners, when clean plates began to appear with each course.

Seventeenth-century Paris was small. It was virtually bounded by the Place de la Bastille in the north-east, and by the Boulevard Saint-Germain in the south. In 1648 it possessed only 23,272 houses and 500,000 inhabitants. It was divided into sixteen *quartiers* (these were increased to twenty in 1702). The aristocracy and the rich bourgeois lived in private *hôtels*, built of stone; the poorer classes lived in wood-and-plaster shacks, where the ground floor was often taken up by shops and stalls.

The Pont-Neuf and the Place Dauphine were the scene of the most lively trade. Pedlars would sell you the latest illicit publication from The Hague, quacks and alchemists would try to persuade you to accept a quick panacea for all your ills, beggars would relieve you, deftly, of any change which the pickpockets had failed to extract. It is estimated that there were forty thousand beggars in Paris alone (almost a tenth of the population). Some parts of Paris were traditionally set aside for the mendicant population. Even the police did not dare to enter them. The city was hazardous after dark, and no prudent citizen would venture out alone and unescorted. The hygiene of the capital left much to be desired. In 1668 La Reynie made primitive sanitation obligatory.

Paris was full of carts and carriages. In 1662 there was an attempt to provide public transport, and the Duc de Roannez set up a service of *carrosses à 5 sols.* These carriages bore coats-of-arms (an attraction to bourgeois passengers), and they started at about half past six in the morning. Their termini were the Luxembourg Gardens, the Porte Saint-Antoine by the Bastille, and Saint-Roch in the Rue Saint-Honoré. On 21 March 1662, a Parisian observer, Mme Périer, reported:

> The thing was so successful that, on the first morning, there were a few women travelling; but after dinner there was such a crowd that one could not get near them, and the other days have been the same. . . . You see a crowd in the streets, waiting for a carriage, but, when it arrives,

The medical profession, satirised by Molière, is mocked again in this caricature of a doctor: a quack, one suspects, who knows more about books than he does about human beings.

it's full. . . . You console yourself, because you know that another carriage is coming in seven and a half minutes. . . . That's full, too!

Despite the enthusiasm of the early days, the carriages were not a complete success, and after four or five years were abandoned.

Another social amenity proved to be more welcome. The reign of Louis XIV saw the birth of the café as a social institution. The first was the Café Procope – which survived to be patronized by Voltaire and Verlaine, and still attracts the visitor today. Fashionable citizens drank tea at the cafés, but cocoa was much cheaper

than tea, and it was drunk by the less affluent. However, in 1671 the fashion abruptly changed: cocoa-drinking was said to be a danger to health, and responsible for all kinds of ailments.

It was wiser not to be ill in the reign of *le Roi Soleil*. Doctors could behave as they liked and charge what they chose. Their training was still tied up with the study of astrology. Treatments were drastic, not to say brutal, and they seem to have been as unscientific as diagnoses. Bleedings, purges and enemas were frequently prescribed, and the most repulsive concoctions were administered to those who asked for professional attention. One book of reference declared that the sovereign remedy for colic was to carry on one's person a silver ring or box which contained a piece of the umbilical cord of a new-born child, and to let the ring touch the flesh. As for the victims of dentistry, they were often bled for toothache. It was not surprising that, like the King, some preferred to treat themselves with cotton-wool soaked in oil of cloves. Others resorted to old wives' remedies, and stuffed the cavity with a mixture of earth-worms and wax.

Such were the conditions of bourgeois life under Louis XIV. As for the poorer classes, they sent their children to the *petites écoles*. In towns, the pupils attended primary schools from eight to eleven in the morning, and from two to five in the afternoon. In the country, education was sometimes non-existent: it was common for children not to attend at all except in winter, for they were needed to help on the farms for the rest of the year. School-mistresses were mostly nuns, but many schoolmasters were laymen chosen by the local inhabitants. These laymen were confirmed in their office by the *intendant* of the district, but the bishop of the diocese had the power to cancel their licence to teach if their moral influence was not to his liking. Superstition was rife in the country. People cursed with the evil eye were said to be everywhere; ghosts were suspected on all sides.

For the humbler subjects of Louis XIV, life was rigorous in the extreme. On 2 September 1661 a doctor, Gui Patin, observed that 'the poor can do nothing but wait for relief; and so they are dying all over France of sickness, misery, oppression, poverty and despair. . . . I think that the Tupinambus are happier in their savage state than the peasants of France are today. The harvest hasn't been good, and wheat will be very dear again. . . .' Early in 1662, the *intendant* of Caen reported to Colbert that there were peasants living only on raw cabbage roots and vegetables. There

This head of a peasant woman comes from a painting by Louis Le Nain of a working family at home. It shows an honest, touching dignity which is not to be found in any portrait of Louis XIV.

'Born for toil' is a fair caption for this engraving of a countryman in *le Grand Siècle*. It was on the labour of such men that the King depended for his revenue, his frequent wars and his display of grandeur.

OPPOSITE Peasant women carrying pails and brooms. An engraving of the period.

were so many people in need that charity was exhausted. There was acute need in Paris, too. In 1662, the Paris working classes sent a petition to the King:

SIRE,

The poor of Paris are very numerous and very needy. They beg Your Majesty to have pity on them. Their misery has reached its depths. They have suffered a thousand ills before they have had recourse to Your Majesty.

Their labour is now useless because trade and all sorts of work have so diminished. They have sold their very clothes. . . .

The parish charities, Sire, can assist them no more, for they are over-

burdened with the sick and ailing, and with orphans. The hospitals are so full that they can take in no more. . . . Where will the poor of Paris go, then? . . . They are condemned to death, if Your Majesty does not give them bread. . . .

When there was work, the working day was often fourteen hours long. At Nevers, towards the end of the century, a stonemason earned twelve to fifteen sous a day, a carpenter's mate earned twelve and a master-craftsman fifteen to eighteen. The miners at Saint-Étienne earned fifteen to sixteen, weavers twelve to fifteen, and Paris locksmiths thirty sous. At Nevers a loaf of bread weighing 430 grammes cost between one and two sous,

FOLLOWING PAGES The baker's cart. From a painting by Michelin (late seventeenth century).

Illustration of the proverb: 'The nobleman is the spider and the peasant is the fly,' by J. Lagnier (1620–72). The nobleman is ready to take everything from the labourer, and to give him nothing in return.

beef cost two or three sous a pound. A servant in Vivarais was paid twenty-four livres a year – and the year's wages were about the price of a pig at the local market.

In provincial France, most houses were made of wood or wood-and-wattle. Most peasant cottages had only one room, with beaten-down earth for a floor, and they had a thatched roof and one window. A simple partition separated this room from the cow-shed, so that the cottage smelled perpetually of manure. Vegetable soup, butter, milk products, bacon and fruit were the principal foods, the peasant almost never ate meat, and he rarely ate poultry. He suffered, too, from shortage of ground, especially after 1669, when the King made it legal for nobles to appropriate lands which had belonged to the communes; the noblemen promptly responded, and took the best fields available.

Life in seventeenth-century France was necessarily hard because scientific discovery had not yet begun to work for man. This was especially true in the country. Farm animals were smaller and thinner than those we know today. The steers gave less beef, the sheep yielded less wool. Since the farmer was often tied to a single crop, he was much more vulnerable. The last years of the great reign failed to bring any alleviation of the plight of the peasants and working people, or to reduce the colossal army of beggars. Taxation increased, and the onset of plagues made provinces desperate. Food shortages led to riots, and riots were ruthlessly suppressed. Little provision was made for social welfare. The peasant and the worker did not belong to recognized or recognizable classes of society.

Henri IV had wanted every peasant in his realm to have a chicken in the pot on Sundays. Louis XIV, in dazzling isolation at Versailles, showed none of the humanity of his ancestor. We are told that his brother undertook to speak to him about the misery of the common people. He received a reply which was worthier of a tiger, if a tiger could talk, than of a Christian King: 'If four or five thousand of that *canaille* were to die, would France be diminished? They are not much use in the world. I pray you, do not meddle in matters which do not concern you.'

L'ÉCOLE DES MARIS

DOM GARCIE ou LE PRINCE JALOUX

L'IMPROMPTU DE VERSAILL

5
The Age of Classicism

THE SEVENTEENTH CENTURY, in France, was an authoritarian century: authoritarian in its politics, in the code which governed the upper classes of society, in its architecture and its art. It was authoritarian, too, in its literature. There were, of course, exceptions. La Fontaine wrote his *Fables* with delectable nonchalance – or so, at least, it appeared from the freedom of his style. His subjects – though they were sanctioned by Aesop – had no other claim to classical lineage. Mme de Sévigné wrote her letters to her daughter without, one suspects, the least shadow of public thought. The topics she discussed, the gossip in which she clearly delighted, could belong only to the age of Louis XIV. But her wit, her freedom of manner, and her human warmth, set her correspondence outside time. In an age of restriction, she wrote with no restrictions except those imposed by instinctive taste and style.

Yet such exceptions serve only to prove the general rule. In the heyday of Louis XIV, literature – like Versailles – represented the spirit of upper-class society. It represented its grandeur, intensity and ordered beauty. It was founded upon a general political and philosophical acceptance; it took for granted a fixed and aristocratic society, and the teaching of the Roman Catholic Church. It lacked the perception of the significance of natural phenomena which dominates the literature of the Romantic revival. Fate, eternity, nature and the destiny of man were mysteries which it almost entirely ignored. To modern readers, accustomed to a searching, comprehensive literature, which has total freedom of style and expression, and so can attempt to treat the largest and deepest themes, French classical literature may at first seem restricted and artificial. English readers, bred on Shakespeare, more inclined by nature to the romantic than the classical, may find that a taste for French literature of the seventeenth century is not easy to acquire. But, with patience, one comes to appreciate its formal charm and penetration. French literature in the reign of Louis XIV was indeed well-ordered. It conformed to classical rules. In doing so, it came close to the French spirit. In no other period have the characteristic features of French intellect and genius – method, logical sequence of ideas and lucidity of style – been so conspicuous. The literary movement which had begun in the days of Richelieu culminated in a blaze of glory.

René Descartes, it must be emphasized, belonged to an earlier generation; his *Discours de la Méthode* had appeared in 1637, and

PREVIOUS PAGES Scenes from plays by Molière. Engraved by an eighteenth-century artist.
OPPOSITE One of the great letter-writers of the French language: Marie de Rabutin-Chantal, Marquise de Sévigné (1626–96).

Domat

Mon pere sest servi de ce corps
de droit pour son ouvrage
des loix civiles

portrait de Mr pascal fait par mon pere

OPPOSITE Blaise Pascal (1623–62), philosopher, physicist and one of the supreme masters of French prose. From a drawing by Domat.

Nicolas Boileau-Despréaux (1636–1711), author of *L'Art Poétique*, and one of the founders of French literary criticism. From the portrait by Hyacinthe Rigaud, now at Versailles.

he died in 1650. But Blaise Pascal, philosopher, physicist and mathematician, was born in 1623, and wrote his two famous works during the reign of Louis XIV. In 1656–7 he published *Lettres provinciales*, in which he discussed divine grace and – a resounding triumph – discredited the ethical code of the Jesuits. During his last years he thought of writing an apologia for Christianity; but the work was never finished, and all that we have are the *Pensées*. Their spirit may be summarized in the words: 'It is the heart that feels God, and not the intellect. That is the meaning of faith: a heart aware of God.' The *Pensées* are remarkable for their analysis of character, and for their combination of powerful reasoning with passionate and lyrical devotion. Pascal died in 1662. The *Pensées* were imperfectly published in 1670. They established him as a pre-eminent religious philosopher, and as one of the greatest masters of French prose.

Nicolas Boileau-Despréaux, better known as Boileau, was born in 1636 and died in 1711. In 1666 he published a complimentary *Discours au Roi*; in about 1669 he was presented to the King, to whom he read his first *Épître*, another complimentary work. He was rewarded with a pension. In 1674 there appeared the edition of his work which contained the famous *L'art poétique*: a summary of the doctrines of contemporary classical writers. Together with Racine, one of his friends, he was appointed a royal historiographer, and in 1684, at the King's insistence, he was elected to the *Académie-Française*.

Boileau recognized, from the first, the merits of Racine and Molière. But he claimed greater distinction. For a long while he persuaded people that he had set Racine and Molière on the right path, and that they owed their masterpieces to him. Boileau also maintained that *L'art poétique* introduced a sort of code into French literature, while in fact it only developed ideas which were already accepted. Boileau persuaded posterity that he had been the first to affirm the principles of classical literature, while in fact all these principles might already be found in Chapelain and in Guez de Balzac. Boileau's rôle was not, in short, to create a doctrine, or to ensure its acceptance. It was to express the ideas of the new classical school: to summarize striking formulas in vigorous verse.

Boileau's reputation may be debatable. No one is likely to question the reputation of his friend Jean-Baptiste Poquelin, known as Molière. Born in Paris in 1622, Molière was the son of an upholsterer. He grew up in his father's workshop in the Rue Saint-Honoré. His mother died when he was ten. He was educated by the Jesuits at the Collège de Clermont, and then studied law. But he soon abandoned the bar and turned to the theatre. He made two attempts to establish a theatre in Paris, and, when they failed, in 1645, he set out for the provinces, which he was to tour for more than twelve years. In 1658 it was announced that he would return to Paris. He duly returned, and gave a performance in the presence of the King. Louis granted him the Salle du Petit-Bourbon as a theatre, and then, from October 1660, the Salle du Palais-Royal. The Salle du Palais-Royal had been built by Richelieu;

The creator of French comedy: Jean-Baptiste Poquelin, known as Molière (1622–73). From the portrait by Pierre Mignard, now at the Théâtre-Français.

it was a beautiful setting for entertainments, but part of the ceiling had collapsed, and until 1671 the audience was protected by a canvas awning. Molière brought two comedies back from the provinces: *L'Étourdi* and *Le Dépit amoureux*. They were Italian in inspiration. In December 1659 he presented a completely original work to the public: *Les Précieuses ridicules*.

Preciosity had been brought into fashion by the *salon* of Mme de Rambouillet. It had originally meant the pursuit of elegance and distinction in manners, style and language; it had entailed the devising of new and metaphorical expressions, the avoidance of low or barbarous words. Preciosity, at its best, was delicacy of taste and feeling, of manners and language. At its worst, it was ludicrous affectation. Its practitioners could not even mention a chair by name: they felt obliged to refer to 'a commodity of conversation'. In *Les Précieuses ridicules*, Molière satirized the *salons* of the *précieuses*, and he did so with devastating effect. The farce enjoyed enormous success. When it was performed again, in the presence of Mazarin and the King, Louis presented its author with £1,000: a handsome sign of satisfaction.

Henceforth, accepted by the public, patronized by the King, Molière steadily pursued his three careers as author, actor and director of a theatrical company. He had to ensure the prosperity of the Théâtre du Palais-Royal and provide the Court, on demand, with the entertainments it required. In December 1662 he presented his second masterpiece, *L'École des Femmes*, which combined comic verve with the philosophy of a moralist. His triumph irritated the rival actors at the Hôtel de Bourgogne, and his boldness of expression antagonized the pious, who leagued against him. The whole of 1663 was filled with what is known as the quarrel of *L'École des Femmes*. However, the King and Boileau were among his supporters, and he answered his adversaries with *La Critique de l'École des Femmes* and *L'Impromptu de Versailles*. He was also preparing a comedy in which he would attack the pious who had criticized his play. On 12 May 1664 he performed the first three acts of *Tartuffe* before the King.

The King's benevolence was not itself enough to ensure the triumph of *Tartuffe*. The Compagnie du Saint-Sacrement immediately set powerful influences to work, and *Tartuffe* was banned. It was only after the death of the pious Anne of Austria, on 5 February 1666, that the play was finally authorized. Molière was turning more and more towards social satire. *L'Amour médecin* (1665) presented the Court physicians on stage. *Le Misanthrope*

OPPOSITE Molière was an actor as well as a dramatist and director. Here he is seen as the eponymous hero of his one-act play, *Sganarelle*.

FOLLOWING PAGES A performance of Molière's comedy, *Le Malade Imaginaire* at Versailles. Louis XIV is seen in the centre of the front row of spectators.

Simonin Fecit
Le vray Portrait de Mr de Moliere en Habit de Sganarelle.

Troisiéme Iournée.
Le Malade imaginaire, Comedie representée
dans le Iardin de Versailles devant la Grotte.

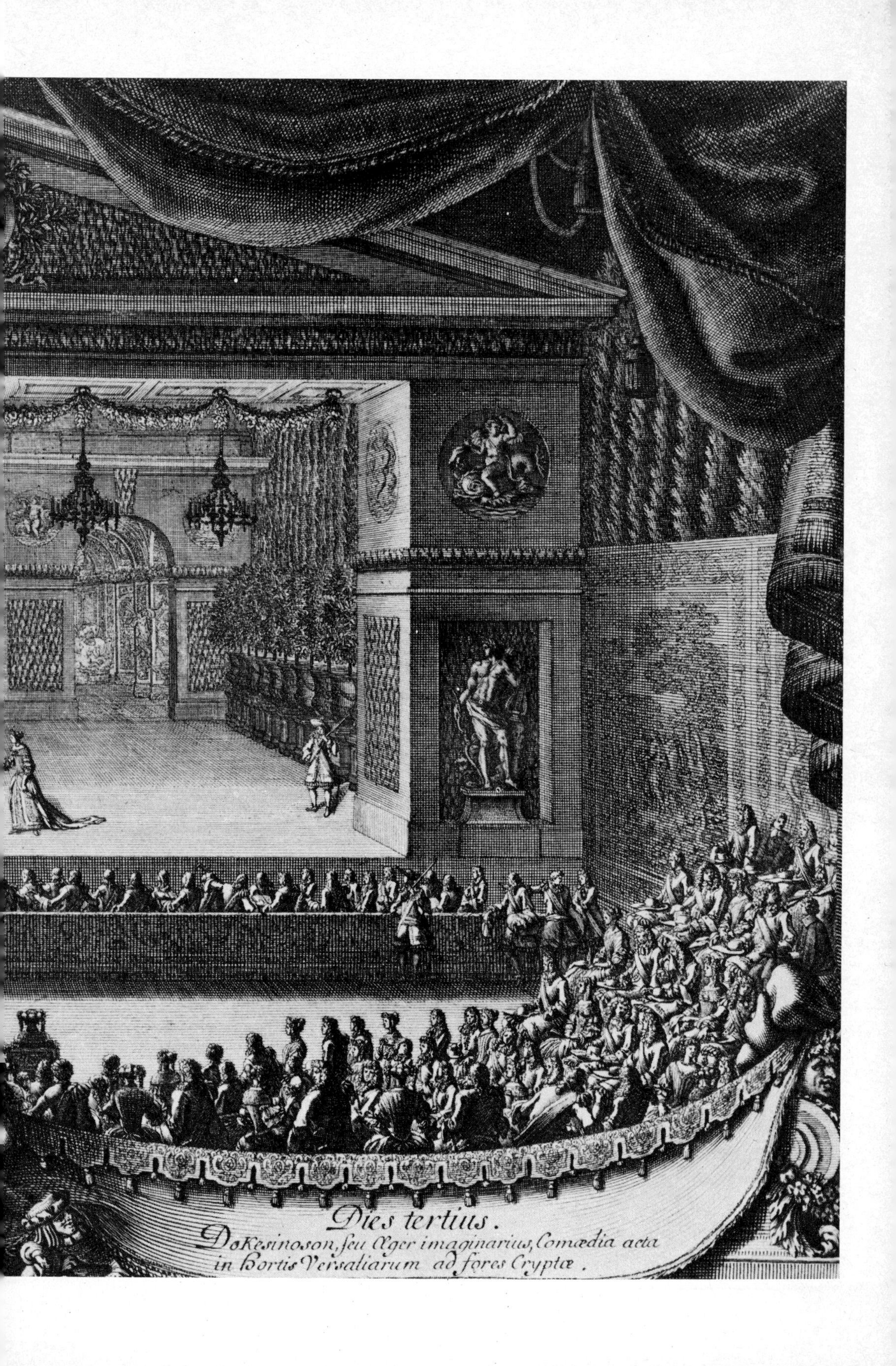
Dies tertius.
Δοκησίνοσον, seu Æger imaginarius, Comœdia acta
in hortis Versaliarum ad fores Cryptæ.

Louis XIV has *déjeuner* with Molière. Whether the incident was apocryphal or not, it inspired this painting by Ingres, now at the Théâtre-Français.

(1666) was both a study of character and a painting of contemporary manners. But the public found this comedy a little serious, and soon afterwards Molière gave them *Le Médecin malgré lui*.

More than once, so we are told, the King himself collaborated with Molière. One day in 1662, a courtier had been listing the succulent courses in a dinner eaten by the King's old tutor, Bishop Péréfixe. As each course was specified, the King remarked indulgently: *'Le pauvre homme!'* Molière overheard, and five

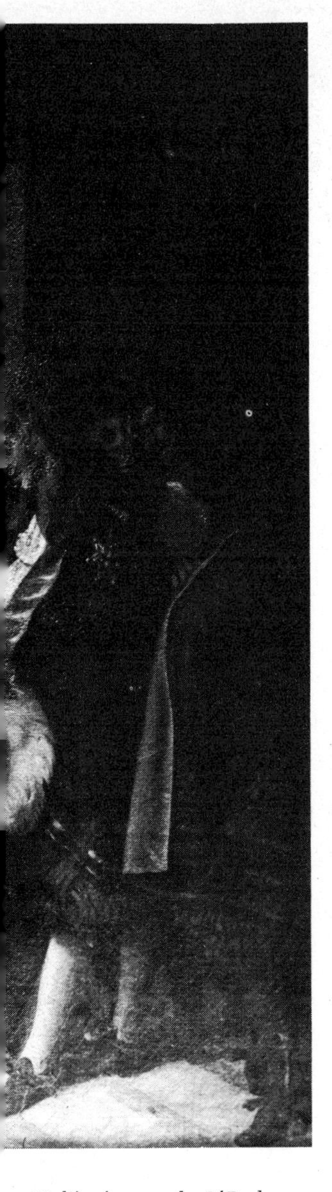

Molière's comedy *L'Ecole des Femmes* aroused controversy; he wrote a one-act comedy, *La Critique de l'Ecole des Femmes*, in which he ridiculed his adversaries. An eighteenth-century artist left this impression of it.

years later he gave the words to Orgon, in *Tartuffe*. Now Louis contributed, more directly, to Molière's work. A French businessman returned from Smyrna and described Turkish customs to the King. Louis immediately thought of introducing Turks on stage. He put the businessman in touch with Molière and Lully. The result was *Le Bourgeois Gentilhomme*, given in 1670, which 'satisfied the King and all the Court'.

There followed *Les Femmes savantes* (1672), and, finally, *Le*

PETRVS CORNELIVS ROTHOMAGENSIS
Anno Dñi. 1643.
M.asne deli. et sc.

Malade imaginaire, which touched – with apparent frivolity – on serious problems. It was first performed at the Palais-Royal on 10 February 1673. On 17 February, at the fourth performance, Molière – who was playing the title rôle – was taken ill on stage. He was carried home where, a few hours later, he died. It is an eloquent comment on the social standing of the actor that the local curate refused him burial; his widow appealed to the King, who intervened. Molière's body was taken to the Cimetière Saint-Joseph, though it was taken there after night-fall.

We must not see Molière simply as a moralist, still less as a defender of modest, bourgeois virtues. He is an artist and a poet. He dreamed of an entertainment in which words, music and dance were closely associated, and more than once he attempted to devise it. He appreciated the resources of popular farce, French and Italian. His taste was wide enough to embrace every form of comic art. He was also a moralist. He attacked with vigour – even with imprudence – all forms of pretension. He wanted his work to give happiness to mankind.

After his death, his company was re-formed under the management of his widow, Armande Béjart; within a few years it managed to rid itself of its rivals by annexing the company of the Théâtre du Marais, and then that of the Hôtel de Bourgogne. Louis XIV decreed that all three companies should be merged into one; and this company, which alone remained to challenge the Comédiens-Italiens, took the name of Comédie-Française. And because this fusion realized the posthumous victory of Molière, the Comédie-Française, the first State theatre of France, is also known as la Maison de Molière.

In depth and penetration and criticism of life, Molière, said Matthew Arnold,

> belongs to the same family as Sophocles and Shakespeare. Corneille and Racine are quite of another order. We must not be misled by the excessive estimate of them among their own countrymen. . . . We English had Shakespeare waiting to open our eyes, whensoever a favourable moment came, to the insufficencies of Pope. But the French had no Shakespeare to open their eyes to the insufficiencies of Corneille and Racine.

The insufficiencies – at least to English eyes – were not those of the dramatists themselves, they were those of the accepted rules. Seventeenth-century drama was bound by the three unities of time, place and action. There could be one action only in a play. It must occur in a single place, and it must do so in the

Pierre Corneille (1606–84) belongs, perhaps, to an earlier age than that of the Sun King, but his tragedies were often compared to those of Racine.

space of twenty-four hours. These arbitrary rules might lead to improbable events: conspirators might have to conspire in the very palace of the king. The rules created awkward dramatic necessities: confidants would have to listen at exhausting length to narratives of what had gone before; messengers would have to bring comprehensive chronicles of actions which had taken place off stage. There was no time to watch the slow development of passions; there was only time to catch the moment of crisis. This must be done in the accepted verse-form, using only the accepted words. Bound by these rigorous and – to us – unnecessary rules, Corneille and Racine wrote their masterpieces.

Pierre Corneille (1606-84) was the son of an advocate in Rouen, and he belongs perhaps to an earlier age than that of the Sun King. His most momentous play, *Le Cid*, was produced in 1637, the year before Louis's birth; *Horace, Cinna* and *Polyeucte* appeared in Louis's infancy. Corneille has a genius for dramatic invention, but his temperament does not easily accept the rigorous demands of tragedy. The Cornelian hero is always led by his concern for glory. Love, to him, is a secondary passion; it can become a noble feeling only if he is already exalted by another ideal. The grandeur of the Cornelian hero often rouses admiration, but it rarely rouses our pity. Corneille's theatre, applauded by the generation of Louis XIII, was less appreciated at the end of the seventeenth century and during the century that followed. It was again successful in the nineteenth century, beginning with the Romantic period. Its power of inspiration – one might even say its Romanticism – was acclaimed, then, at the expense of the 'classical' sobriety of Racine.

Jean Racine, born in 1639, was virtually Louis's contemporary. His mother died when he was only thirteen months old, and his father died when the child was four. They left him no money, and the nuns at Port-Royal, to whom his family had shown devotion, took it upon themselves to educate him. He went on to the college at Beauvais, which was a centre of Jansenism, and he stayed there until 1655. Then he was educated at the schools of Port-Royal, where he acquired not only the Jansenist doctrines but a wide knowledge of Greek and Latin literature. In 1658 he went to the Collège d'Harcourt, in the University of Paris. He was already writing poetry, and, in 1660, *La Nymphe de la Seine* was much appreciated. That year, and in 1661, he wrote two tragedies which were not performed and have since been lost.

For a moment Racine thought of an ecclesiastical career, but he

Corneille's tragedy *Horace* was first produced in 1640; this illustration of a scene comes from a seventeenth-century edition of the work.

C'eſt trop, ma paſſion à la raiſon fait place.
Va dedans les enfers plaindre ton Curiace.

OPPOSITE This drawing of Jean Racine (1639–99) was made by his eldest son.

BELOW This frontispiece was designed by Charles Le Brun for the first edition of the works of Racine, published in 1672.

BELOW RIGHT Racine's *Bérénice* was produced in 1670. It was considered superior to Corneille's *Tite et Bérénice*.

soon realized his error, and late in 1662, or early in 1663, he returned to Paris, where once again he turned to the theatre. His first play, *La Thébaïde*, had little success; but *Alexandre* (December 1665) set him in the first rank of contemporary authors. He had made the acquaintance of Boileau (who exercised considerable influence over him), and he had known La Fontaine for some years. He also knew Molière for a time: indeed, Molière had produced *La Thébaïde*. In 1665, Racine showed him shocking ingratitude by giving *Alexandre* to his rivals at the Hôtel de Bourgogne. There was, understandably, a breach between them.

The period of masterpieces began in 1667, with *Andromaque*. This was followed by *Les Plaideurs* (1669), *Bérénice* (1670), *Mithridate* (1673). *Iphigénie* (1675) and *Phèdre* (1677). Racine was soon considered the greatest writer of tragedy of the day.

Racine
Dessiné par
son fils aîné.

The only people to resist his triumph were the partisans of the ageing Corneille, who remained faithful to the taste of their youth. The Court, especially, was all for Racine; Mme de Montespan, then at the height of her favour, patronized him in striking fashion. The King himself was so fond of him that he gave him lodgings at Versailles, and free access to him whenever he wished to come. In the later years of his reign, he would listen to him reading his works.

The public was therefore astonished to learn, in 1677, that Racine had stopped writing tragedies. There were several reasons for this decision. Louis XIV had recently appointed him one of the royal historiographers, and this official task was hardly compatible with the trade of poet. Racine and his fellow-historiographer, Boileau, were expected to celebrate the royal victories. Racine took his duties seriously, and accompanied the King on journeys and on military expeditions. On one occasion, we are told, the King met him at Court, and expressed his regret that Racine had not come on his last campaign. Racine was nothing if not a courtier. 'Sire,' he replied, 'Monsieur Boileau and I had only our town dress. We had ordered country clothes, but the places you were attacking fell before our clothes were finished.'

There were two other reasons why Racine abandoned tragedy. In 1665 he had quarrelled with Port-Royal, but he had now returned to the austere principles of his old teachers. He was also profoundly affected by the cabal which was formed against *Phèdre*.

Twelve years later he returned to the theatre. In 1689 he wrote *Esther*, and in 1691 he wrote *Athalie*, at the request of Mme de Maintenon, for the young girls at Saint-Cyr. Once again the party of piety showed itself hostile to the theatre; it persuaded Mme de Maintenon that *Athalie* should not be performed. The rehearsals were broken off, and Racine ceased to write religious tragedies. He lived as an austere Christian, concerned with the education of his children, but he did not hide his faithfulness to Port-Royal. He was not disgraced, but his favour waned. He died on 21 April 1699.

In their main features, Racine's tragedies follow those of Corneille; but they differ in certain important respects. They do not present the will triumphant over instinct and circumstance, they show it to be weak and vacillating (and here, perhaps, we may detect the Jansenist influence). Racine's characters are more real and human than those of Corneille. His most striking charac-

A scene from Racine's *Esther*, first produced in 1689.

ters are women, and it has been said that he inaugurated the literature of the passions of the heart. Corneille had painted men as they should be, Racine painted them as they were. Critics have rightly admired the ease with which Racine observes the rules of classical drama. We should perhaps admire even more the beauty of Racinian dialogue, its purity, its poetry, its attempt to rediscover the grandeur of the Greek poets.

Jean de La Fontaine, poet and fabulist, was less fortunate in his career. He was born in 1621 at Château-Thierry in Champagne, where his father held a post in the administration of the *Eaux et Forêts*. He received part of his education at an Oratorian college in Paris, and for a while he considered entering the Church. Then he studied law; but he showed no inclination for work, and was content to spend ten years in idleness in his native town, and most of the remainder of his life as the pensioner of wealthy patrons. He married in 1647 and had a son, but the marriage ended, almost predictably, in separation. In 1652 he inherited his father's appointment as *Maître des Eaux et Forêts*, but relinquished it. His work, incidentally, did not prevent him from continuing to lead a nonchalant life, nor did it solve his financial problems.

In 1654 he made his literary début with an imitation of the *Eunuchus* of Terence. Two years later he became a pensioner of Fouquet, for whom he wrote light verses, the more weighty poem *Adonis* and the comedy *Clymène*. After the Minister's disgrace in 1661, La Fontaine wrote his *Élégie aux Nymphes de Vaux*, asking them to beg the King for clemency for his patron. The prayer of La Fontaine and the nymphs remained unanswered.

However, after Fouquet's disgrace, La Fontaine had other patrons; among them was Madame, the widow of Gaston d'Orléans. In 1664 she appointed him one of her gentlemen in attendance. From this period we may date the first collections of *Contes* (1665, 1666, 1671), the first six books of the *Fables* (1668), *Psyché* (1669), two new collections of *Contes* (1671-4) and the *Fables* now collected in Books VII to XI (1678-9). These last were brilliantly successful. La Fontaine was elected to the *Académie-Française* in 1683, but he waited until 1684 for the approval of the King, who wanted Boileau to be admitted first. In 1694, the year before his death, La Fontaine published a last book of *Fables*. They were dedicated to the King's grandson, the Duc de Bourgogne.

The *Contes* are inspired by the sometimes licentious Gaulois tradition, but they reveal La Fontaine's peculiar charm. The narratives are lively, alert and full of humour; they were labor-

A tribute to the poet and fabulist Jean de La Fontaine (1621–95). An engraving by Jean-Baptiste Oudry, the animal painter.

iously written, but the rhythm and melody of the lines give them an appearance of complete and astonishing ease of manner. In the *Fables*, on which his fame must rest, La Fontaine endows the old tales with remarkable vividness. He observes the world shrewdly, with disillusioned wisdom. Weak and feckless, he was a man of keen intelligence and poetic genius, who perfectly described himself as 'a butterfly on Parnassus'.

The age was great in prose as well as poetry, and one of its masters was Jacques-Bénigne Bossuet, Bishop of Meaux. He represented the best and most serious elements in the Court of Louis XIV. But if he saw all round his age, he did not see beyond it. The order of things under Louis XIV was, to him, the one order; beyond that, the whole universe was confusion, heresy and the work of Satan. Yet if Bossuet's thinking was limited, his style was magnificent. He was famous for the educational works which he prepared for his pupil, the King's son, *le Grand Dauphin*; he was famous, above all, for his funeral orations. One may still imagine the effect of his oration on the death of Henriette, the sister-in-law of the King. She had died prematurely, and she had been much loved. 'Oh, fateful night! Oh, dreadful night, when, suddenly, like a clap of thunder, there echoed that astounding news: Madame is dying, Madame is dead!'

In fact the prestige of Bossuet comes from his oratorical genius. He created a personal style, compounded of grandeur and simplicity; this 'natural' eloquence relates him to the great masters of Classicism. He composed the draft of his sermon as near as possible to the moment when he was to deliver it; then he put down a few striking images on paper. This immediacy and improvisation explains the warmth and movement of his sermons. His finest funeral orations are admirable pictures of princely lives, the grandiose illustration of the picture which he drew of destiny: noble enterprises, brilliant triumphs and death in which all human things must end.

Bossuet was known as the Eagle of Meaux. François de Salignac de la Mothe-Fénelon was known as the Swan of Cambrai. Born in 1651, of an old Gascon family, he received a sound classical education, became a priest and a disciple of Bossuet. In 1678 he was appointed Superior of certain convents in Paris, and after the Revocation of the Edict of Nantes, in 1685, he helped to convert the Huguenots in the west of France – or, as Mme de Sévigné mildly observed, 'to perfect the work done by the dragoons'. He became the spiritual leader of a devout group at Court, and he

Jacques-Bénigne Bossuet, Bishop of Meaux (1627–1704) was famous for his sermons and funeral orations and for the educational works which he prepared for his pupil *le Grand Dauphin*, son of Louis XIV. Pupil and tutor are seen together in this engraving.

was favoured by Mme de Maintenon. In 1689 he was charged with the education of the King's grandson. The Duc de Bourgogne was a difficult pupil, but Fénelon transformed him. His appointment brought him election to the *Académie-Française* in 1693 and, two years later, the archbishopric of Cambrai. But soon his triumphal career was checked; religious controversy alienated him from Mme de Maintenon and the King. In 1699 *Télémaque* completed his disgrace. Fénelon had written this didactic romance for his pupil, and it contained criticisms of the government of Louis XIV. Fénelon was deprived of his preceptorate and relegated to Cambrai, where he died, unpardoned, in 1715.

Realist and mystic, ambitious but disinterested, Fénelon is made up of contrasts; his political idealism and fear of despotism already suggest the attitude of the eighteenth-century *philosophes*, but he remains a great lord, proud of his nobility.

Two other critics of the régime must be mentioned. François VI, Duc de La Rochefoucauld, was born in 1613; before he was fifteen, he married the daughter of a Great Falconer of France. After a military career, he went to Court, where he became involved in intrigues: indeed, he became so involved that he found himself obliged to cool his heels in the Bastille, and to spend two years in exile on his estates. In 1642 he returned to Court, where he intrigued more than ever. He took an active part in the Fronde in 1646 and, two years later, in the *Fronde des princes,* with the title of Lieutenant-General of the rebel army. In 1652 he was gravely wounded, but the following year he rallied to the King; thenceforth he led a purely social life. In 1659 the magnanimous Louis granted him a pension. In 1664, at The Hague, the royal pensioner published his *Réflexions ou sentences et maximes morales.* The *Maximes*, as the work was generally called, was republished in Paris the following year, and went into several editions. It is a collection of some five hundred sentences in which the author analyses human conduct with ruthless penetration. La Rochefoucauld's bitter and pessimistic philosophy had a wide influence; and Voltaire, who admired the precision of his style, said that he contributed greatly to form the taste of the nation. La Rochefoucauld died in 1680; his *Réflexions diverses* did not appear until long after his death.

François de Salignac de la Mothe-Fénelon (1651–1715): theologian, Archbishop of Cambrai and tutor of the King's grandson, the Duc de Bourgogne.

Jean de La Bruyère was born in 1645, the son of a controller-general of incomes in the City of Paris. He graduated in law at the university of Orléans, and he was called to the bar, but he did little pleading; and in 1673 he bought the functions of

treasurer-general of France in the *généralité* of Caen (he was to sell the functions in 1686). In 1684, on the recommendation of Bossuet, he was summoned to Chantilly to teach history to the grandson of the great Condé; and, when his task was finished, he remained in the household of the Condés as a gentleman and secretary. He could therefore approach the world of the Court, and it was an excellent observation post for him.

In 1688, he published the *Caractères de Théophraste traduits du grec, avec les caractères et les mœurs de ce siècle.* La Bruyère's work was simply presented as a kind of appendix to a translation from the Greek moralist, but it was a triumphant success. From the fourth edition (1689) to the ninth, in 1696, La Bruyère constantly enlarged it. He was elected to the *Académie-Française* in 1693, three years before his death.

In his *Caractères*, with sober scorn, he passes judgment on the vanity and the frivolity of those about him. The work consists largely of observations on character and conduct, interspersed with portraits. The success of the *Caractères* is due largely to the portraits, many of them of living people who are presented under pseudonyms. They exemplify the failings which La Bruyère describes. People published editions of the work with names and keys. La Bruyère protested that any likenesses were purely accidental, but he protested in vain. He painted French society at a time when it was being profoundly transformed. He noted the external features, but he recognized the political and moral causes. The public was conquered. In the *Caractères*, Versailles rises before us: not so much its outward form as its secret, essential self. And the judgment which La Bruyère passes on his vision is one of withering scorn. His description of Mass at Versailles, when all the courtiers turned their faces to the King's throne and their backs to the altar of God, shows a spirit very different from that of Bossuet – a spirit not far removed from the undermining criticism of the eighteenth century itself.

Jean de La Bruyère (1645–96), author of the *Caractères*, in which he brilliantly criticized his contemporaries.

6

The Years of Conquest

THERE WAS MUCH TO CRITICIZE in the reign of *le Roi Soleil*. The misery of the masses continued, but the King was possessed by increasing *folie de grandeur*. Like General de Gaulle, three centuries later, he had small concern for the everyday needs of his people – but he had 'a certain idea of France', and this idea involved an unrelenting search for glory. 'My dominant passion is certainly love of glory.' So he wrote at the age of thirty. Love of glory was probably the strongest motive force in seventeenth-century France; and, despite his foreign blood, Louis was a typical Frenchman of the period.

He expressed his love of glory in the creation of Versailles. He expressed it in his conquest of women; and 'his Amours', we are told, 'have made a very great Noise in the world, which is not to be wondered at if the Rank and humour of the Gallant be considered'. Louis also wanted to express his love of *la gloire* by winning military victories and by extending the frontiers of France. This kind of glory he eagerly desired. In 1665 the death of his father-in-law, Philip of Spain, allowed Louis to make a grand gesture. Two years later, he asserted the Queen's rights in the Low Countries, and he annexed part of the Spanish Netherlands as compensation for her unpaid dowry. The Treaty of the Pyrenees had borne belated fruit. Mazarin's foresight had been rewarded. But Louis did not know when to cease aggression. He then alarmed Europe by seizing another Spanish possession, Franche-Comté; and England, Holland and Sweden formed the Triple Alliance against him. The War of Devolution ended in 1668, with the Treaty of Aix-la-Chapelle.

The Treaty made Flanders part of France, and the occasion was celebrated at Versailles. There was a ballet by Lully, *Le Triomphe de Bacchus*, a great ball and a firework display, this last described by the King's historiographer, Félibien des Avaux:

By a prodigious transformation, the château appeared to be the very palace of the Sun. All the intersections of the avenues were suddenly illuminated by antique statues of every hue. In an instant, all the balustrades were bordered with flaming urns which at once decorated and illumined the vast reaches of this magnificent park. Suddenly one heard an almost heroic harmony: the explosion of a thousand fireworks, followed immediately by a thousand plumes of fire soaring up from the fountains.

PREVIOUS PAGES Louis XIV and Maria Teresa enter Arras. This painting, by Van der Meulen, gives some idea of the pomp and circumstance which surrounded the Sun King.

The Marquis de Saint-Maurice was less impressed by the spectacle:

Never [he wrote] have such beautiful water and firework displays been seen. They have cost the King more than 500,000 livres. Everyone says that he would have done better to give this money to the demobilized soldiers. The ladies and gentlemen of quality have also made excessive expenditures in their private capacity; some have spent as much as 15,000 livres on French point-lace: one merchant has sold 80,000 livres' worth. I have had to spend nearly 4,000 livres on adorning myself, my wife, my daughter and her children, and in my opinion I have never spent money so uselessly; I console myself with the thought that when one is among madmen one must be mad oneself.

It seemed, at times, to dispassionate observers, that the King had indeed taken leave of his senses. The Treaty of Aix-la-Chapelle had given him Flanders; it had also obliged him to resign some of his conquests. In the late 1660s he was therefore still in search of glory, and he began to plan a war against Holland. On 6 April 1672, he ordered his well-trained and well-equipped army to invade the United Provinces.

At first the troops advanced quite easily; but long before they reached the frontiers, the Dutch had planned to save themselves by flooding. In the second half of June they began to pierce their walls and dykes; and, as Louis regrouped his army after the fall of Utrecht, he found himself facing a virtual sea. It must have seemed to him that the elements were conspiring against him. In 1673 Spain entered the war on the side of Holland, together with Denmark, Lorraine, Trier and Mainz. The Allies were committed by treaty to continue the war until Louis ceded all his gains since 1672.

He had no intention of doing so. Colbert had wanted war with Holland for commercial reasons, and Louvois, the Minister of War, had wanted it for military prestige. It became a struggle against a defensive coalition of Europe, and the struggle lasted for six years. At the Peace of Nijmegen, in 1678, Louis obtained all that France desired. The Pyrenees and the Alps were secure frontiers to the south and the south-east; a powerful navy defended the coast in the Mediterranean, the Atlantic and the English Channel. The Spanish Netherlands had been largely absorbed, and the safety of Paris was assured by strongly fortified border towns. Now that Franche-Comté was in French hands, the Spanish line of communication between Milan and the Low Countries had been cut. Louis had only to wait until the death of Charles II of Spain allowed him to force the division of the Spanish inheritance on his own terms. What in fact he did was to carry the frontier of France to the Rhine, and in doing so he passed the point where

Louis XIV declaring war against Holland. In this picture by an artist of the school of Charles Le Brun, he is encouraged by the goddesses of War, Justice and Peace. He himself has become an almost mythological figure.

the defence of French interests became defiance of other nations.

The Treaty of Nijmegen marked the apogee of Louis XIV. The French army had proved its merits on the battlefield, French diplomacy was brilliant and Louis's Court attracted visitors, not only from Europe, but from Africa and the East. The influence of Versailles can be seen in the ruins of the Summer Palace of the Manchu Emperors of China.

It was small wonder if the French showed excessive devotion to their sovereign. The historian Pellissier called him 'a visible miracle'; and La Feuillade led his regiment of guards three times round the statue which he had erected to the King in the Place des Victoires in Paris. He made 'all those protestations which in old times the pagans used before the statues of their Emperors'. There was, so we learn, no woman of position who did not aspire to be the King's mistress. Primi Visconti wrote that 'numbers of women, both married and single, have told me that this would not offend either their husbands or their fathers, or even God Himself'.

English observers were less admiring. In 1709, the author of *The Life and History of Lewis XIV* had some harsh observations to make:

> The Cruelties of his Reign are Innumerable, and Black as Hell itself: But . . . he was never taught Obedience to any other Law but that of his Interest and his Will. . . .
>
> His Vanity is proportionable to his Ambition, and that is Unbounded as the Desires of the Soul of Man can be. For he has not only suffer'd, but encourag'd the erecting of Statues, and making of Inscriptions and Devices upon them, which can hardly be outdone by the *Pagan* Antiquity; and which, however taking it may be with the ignorant Sort of that Airy Nation, yet must infinitely disgust all Impartial Men. . . .
>
> No *French* Prince has ever been more Magnificent than he, and indeed since *Charlemagn* none has had the means to be so: Of which the famous Carrousel in 1662, the Palaces of *Versailles, Marli, the Louvre,* and several others built or establish'd by him, are sufficient Evidences. . . .
>
> Nor was that Scepter ever wielded by a Prince, who better understood the Art of Commanding nor had an Education more unfit to qualify him for it.

Louis XIV on horseback. This portrait comes, again, from the studio of Charles Le Brun; it was probably painted in 1668, the year of Louis's triumphal entry into Douai during the French invasion of the Spanish Netherlands.

Louis XIV had been taught much about the art and profession of kingship. He had been given religious guidance, and he had been instructed in fencing, riding, shooting and dancing. Ballet had been brought to France by Catherine de Médicis, the Italian con-

sort of Henri II. Or, rather, she had brought a spectacle which was a combination of dancing, singing and recitation. Ballet, in the form we know, had its official being when in 1661 Louis founded the National Academy of Dancing. He himself, an expert dancer, created many rôles, from comic characters to the gods and heroes of antiquity. He enjoyed the collaboration of the greatest men of his day. Molière conceived subjects for ballets, and advised in their production, and Jean-Baptiste Lully was one of the Court dancing-masters. Under the aegis of Lully – the creator of French national opera – the ballet became professional. In 1669 Louis grew corpulent, and abandoned dancing, and the Court followed suit.

But, whatever his social accomplishments, Louis's formal education had been rudimentary; he often laughed about his ignorance, and, if we are to believe the comments he made in his old age, he was virtually self-educated. Saint-Simon considered that the King was an ignoramus who did not even know how little he knew. His sister-in-law said that he was ashamed of his ignorance, and courtiers were obliged to ridicule scholarship if they wished to please him. He was, in fact, largely ignorant of the classics, but he wrote and spoke French with a certain elegance. He seems to have been quite ignorant of English and German, but he knew enough Italian to speak it fluently and to appreciate Italian lyric poetry; he also learned, imperfectly, to speak Spanish. As a youth, he had never travelled outside his kingdom, but his knowledge of geography was considerable. No doubt he had learned something of art from Mazarin's superb collections; but his knowledge of mathematics and of literature was limited.

He was aware of his limitations, and avid for information. 'My intention is', he wrote, 'to be informed of all that is best and exquisite in all countries and in all branches of knowledge, and to make the best of such information for my honour, and service, and glory.' In this he was, no doubt, marvellously aided and encouraged by Colbert.

And so the years of splendour and euphoria continued. Grimani, the Venetian ambassador, left an account of Louis XIV in the year 1664-5:

> His constitution is sturdy and his appearance majestic, his manner courteous and serious. . . . He evinces partiality to no-one, and no-one can presume on receiving it; he does not let anybody jest with him, nor does he jest with others . . . As he applies himself to work with extra-

ordinary zeal, . . . he fatigues his mind too much and occasionally falls prey to violent headaches. These troubles are accompanied by a certain weakness of the stomach, and he is also subject to dizzy spells and vapours. Hence . . . he has recourse to purges, baths and repeated blood-lettings. . . . As for his mental qualities, his Majesty has natural wisdom and an extremely lucid intelligence. He greets any and everybody with immense goodwill, and in his every action mingles kindness and gravity with a grace that captures every heart. . . .

The King's heart is completely ablaze with two consuming subjects: one is jealousy of his own greatness which rules out any favourite. . . . The other is the desire to surpass, with acts of true magnificence, the finest examples that present themselves for his emulation. . . . His Majesty proceeds with the utmost wisdom in all the affairs of his realm. He can obviously keep a tight curb on his tongue, and never let slip an unconsidered word.

Louis's appetites remained unrestrained, but in other ways he was completely master of himself. He had one supremely important gift, and that was his perfect manner: he was always dignified and courteous. He had the rare gift of saying the right thing at the right moment. When the elderly Condé returned from one of his last campaigns, he went to pay his respects at Saint-Germain. Louis stood at the top of the stairs, surrounded by his Court, and Condé apologized for his slowness in mounting the stairs. 'My cousin,' said Louis, 'one cannot walk fast when one is so burdened with laurels.'

Louis's social grace was proverbial. Even his enemy the Duc de Saint-Simon felt obliged to admire the royal manner:

Never did any man give with a better grace, and thus increase the value of his bounty. Never did a man sell his words, his smile, even his glances in a finer manner. He made everything precious through the discrimination and majesty which were greatly enhanced by the rarity and brevity of his words. . . . Never was there a man so naturally polite, nor of such strictly measured politeness, strict by degrees, nor who better distinguished age, merit, rank. . . . But, above all, he had no equal with women. He never passed by the most modest coif without raising his hat, even to chambermaids. . . . Nothing could match him at reviews, fêtes, and wherever an air of gallantry could be assumed because of the presence of ladies. . . . But to the least gesture, his walk, his bearing, his whole countenance was measured, all seemly, noble, grand, majestic and withal very natural, for habit and the incomparable advantage of his whole figure made all this very easy.

Louis's appearance in the middle years of his reign was recorded more than once by Le Brun, and it was superbly recorded by Bernini. He made amends for his average height (5 feet 6½ inches) by wearing high heels and a towering perruque. He came to give his person a natural and majestic gravity. He personified regality. He was an absolute monarch at a time before that concept was derided: a monarch who recognized that he was made of a different clay from other men. It was, said Primi Visconti, 'a fine sight to see him leave the château with his bodyguards, carriages, horses, courtiers, valets, and a multitude of people all in confusion, bustling noisily around him. It reminds me of the queen bee, going out into the fields with her swarm.' Visconti also observed the difference between the public and the private person: the royal sense of acting a part.

> The King [he wrote] is full of gravity and very different from what he is in his private life. Finding myself in his room with other courtiers, I have noticed more than once that if by chance the door was opened, or if he went out, he immediately composed his attitude and assumed another facial expression, as if he were about to appear on stage; in fact he knows very well how to play the King in everything.

The leading actor remained unchanged; the Court itself was changing. New faces were appearing, and old faces were disappearing from the scene. Louis's mother, Anne of Austria, had died in 1666. His existence as an independent man began only after her death. He had always admired her, and he had always been careful not to offend her: his mistresses and bastards were kept out of her way. As soon as she died, he recognized Louise de La Vallière as his titular mistress, and legitimized their daughter, Marie-Anne.

In October 1666, Louise gave birth to another daughter in the Hôtel Brion, a little house which he had bought her in the grounds of the Palais-Royal. The child was hurried away to its foster-mother. The King often visited Louise at the Hôtel Brion. He had felt for her what was probably the purest passion in his life. And indeed this was not surprising; for, as the Abbé de Choisy observed, Louise de La Vallière 'was extraordinarily lovable. . . . For the rest, not very witty, though she polished her mind every day by assiduous reading. No ambition, no points of view, more apt to dream about the object of her love than to please him, completely enclosed in herself and in her passion, the sole passion of her life.' It was understandable that she had been Louis's first mistress; but he had now begun to tire of her simplicity. In her

Anne of Austria, mother of Louis XIV. Her jewels and her fan seem unusual apparel for a horsewoman.

innocence, and in her genuine love for the King, she invited a friend to the Hôtel Brion: a friend who was quite sure to entertain him.

Madame de Montespan, by a seventeenth-century French artist. The King's mistress is shown as Iris, messenger of the gods, who was changed by Juno into a rainbow.

Athénaïs de Montespan was brilliantly amusing. She was twenty-six, dark-haired, blue-eyed, and endowed with a handsome figure. She was the daughter of Gabriel de Rochechouart, Marquis de Mortemart, Prince de Tonnay-Charente, and she belonged to one of the oldest families in France. She was proud, and she was extravagant (though far from rich). She was the wife of a wild Gascon, Louis, Marquis de Montespan and the mother of two children. She was ambitious and ruthless, and she was experienced; and she knew how to wait. Throughout October she continued to entertain the King at the Hôtel Brion. On 5 November a rumour circulated at Court that he had 'noticed' her.

In May 1667, Louis left Saint-Germain to spend the summer with his army. With him went the Queen and her ladies-in-waiting, including Athénaïs de Montespan. Louise de La Vallière did not go, for she was once again pregnant. Louis created her a duchess: the title was like a parting present given to an old servant. He had inevitably fallen in love with Mme de Montespan, but she felt it expedient to keep him waiting; and it was probably not until the following summer, 1668, that she finally became his mistress.

The Marquis de Montespan, far from complaisant, came to Paris to create a scene. The result was described in a contemporary chronicle, *The Amorous Conquests of the Great Alcander, or, the Amours of the French King, and Madam Montespan.* Although, we are told, the Marquis 'tenderly loved' his wife,

> he did not refrain from giving her a good box on the Ear. Madam de *Montespan,* who well knew where to find support, gave him extream ill Language, and having complain'd of his proceeding to the Great *Alcander*; he banished Monsieur *de Montespan* the Court, who with his Children departed into his own Country, bordering upon the *Pireneans*. . . . And he being much indebted, the Great *Alcander* sent him two thousand Livres, to comfort him for the loss which he had been the occasion of.

In March 1669, when he heard that his wife had given birth to a child by the King, the Marquis informed his friends of 'the death of my wife from coquetry and ambition', and invited them to a mock funeral.

Athénaïs settled down to enjoy her glory – and to exploit it. She coaxed the King into giving her jewels; she persuaded him to give her money, with which she bought a house near the Louvre.

She arranged for her father to be Governor of Paris. She constantly devised new means of holding the King's love. And, for six years – which was still more remarkable – she contrived to keep on civil terms with Louise de La Vallière. Louise had been in many ways singularly unfitted to maintain her position at Court. Her conscience was not easy; the religious life had always attracted her. And now, at last, when she found a rival preferred to herself, it was chiefly her love for the King which made her regret the change.

In his private life, it must be said, Louis behaved abominably. He had proclaimed Louise to be his official mistress at the very moment when he was losing interest in her. Loaded with honours, but out of favour, she had to live for years alongside her victorious rival in order to preserve a few shreds of appearance – for Louis was engaged in double adultery. When the two women travelled, they shared the carriage of the heartbroken Maria Teresa, and onlookers asked one another whether they had seen 'the three Queens'.

In 1674 Louise finally asked the King's permission to become a nun. He granted it. On 18 April she said good-bye to her friends at Court, and asked Maria Teresa for her forgiveness. She dined with Louis and Mme de Montespan. Next day, after Mass, she left in her duchess's coach for the Carmelite convent in the Rue Saint-Jacques. For the rest of her long life – another thirty-six years – she was to be Sister Louise de la Miséricorde. Mme de Scudéry was present when, on 4 June, Louise de La Vallière took the veil. 'She performed the action with much piety', she wrote. 'I think she never looked more beautiful or more content. She should be happy if only because she no longer has to lace up Mme de Montespan's stays. If the truth be told, she was a real Martyr.'

The King now became more generous than ever to Athénaïs. She wanted her own château; but when, on Louis's orders, Mansard drew up plans for a country house, she considered them 'only fit for a chorus girl'. Louis thereupon gave her Clagny, near Versailles; it took ten years to build, and it cost nearly a million pounds. Mme de Sévigné reported: 'You cannot imagine the extent of her triumph, surrounded by her workmen, who number twelve hundred. The palace of Apollidonus and the gardens of Armida combined may give some faint indication of the beauty of this place. The wife of her steadfast friend (i.e. the Queen) visits her, as do the rest of the royal family in turn. She is elevated above all

OPPOSITE Mlle de La Vallière, the King's former mistress, after she had taken the veil. From a painting by Pierre Mignard.

French and Italian actors in an imaginary scene, with Molière on the left. An act could not continue without interruption for longer than it took the candles to burn out. From a painting by an unknown artist.

Le Capitan Matamore

Jodelet *Turlupin*

Molière *Poisson* *Arlequ*

Gros Guillaume *Gaultier Garguille* *polichinelle*
lot Gorju *Pantalon* *Philippin* *Briguelle* *Trivelin*
Le Dottor Grazian Balourd *Scaramouche*

LE PORTRAIT DE LA VOISIN.
Source de tant de maux maudite creature
Qui par mille poisons déstruisois la Nature,
Si la parque en fillant tes detestablés jours
A fait regner la Mort, en prolongeant leur cours,
Vn suplice effroyable et plein d'Ignominie
A sceu trancher le fil de ton énorme vie.
A.C. in.
Chasteau, ex. C.P.R.

the duchesses, that is a fact.' Athénaïs's taste for luxury appeared in the garden at Clagny, which was planted with eight thousand jonquils, and in the farm which, said Mme de Sévigné, was stocked with 'the most passionate turtle doves to be found, the fattest sows, . . . the sheep with the curliest wool, and the goosiest possible geese'.

As Athénais entered her ninth year as 'the second wife of the King', the Court began to wonder how she kept him physically enslaved. The royal physician noted that he often complained of headaches and fits of dizziness. Yet she seemed to have some uncanny power of arousing his passion, and she bore him seven children. It is true that Louis was not entirely faithful to her: at times his attention wandered to Mlle des Oiletts, and to the Princesse de Soubise ('the vision of Mme de Soubise', wrote Mme de Sévigné, 'passed by quicker than a flash of lightning'). The King also looked with favour on Mlle de Ludres and Mlle de Fontanges. But always, in the end, Athénaïs triumphed.

Suddenly, in January 1680, a bombshell burst upon the Court. The Paris police had arrested a number of people accused of poisoning. A special Commission had taken evidence in secret; the Commission now ordered the arrest of six leading lights at Court, including Mazarin's niece, Olympe de Soissons. The chief among the accused was a middle-aged woman, Catherine Monvoisin. La Voisin – as she was called – had provided her clients with love-philtres, and occasionally with poisons to rid them of unwanted husbands. She had celebrated black masses, even sacrificed children, to ensure her clients' success. La Voisin was found guilty and she was burned at the stake. 'I'm just going to tell you about Mme Voisin', Mme de Sévigné explained to her daughter on 23 February. 'She wasn't burnt on Wednesday, as I had told you, it was only yesterday, . . . and her ashes are in the air as I write.' After La Voisin's execution, her daughter Marguerite gave evidence. In the summer of 1680 she claimed that her mother's clients had included Mme de Montespan.

> On several occasions [she confessed], on my mother's orders, I delivered powders to Mme de Montespan which had previously been sprinkled with the chalice, and other powders of whose composition I know nothing, because when I asked what I was to say when handing them over my mother told me to say nothing because all had already been said. Once I saw her concoct a preparation, and it consisted of powdered moles.

La Reynie, the Lieutenant of Police, summed up the charges

One of the most scandalous figures of the reign: La Voisin, poisoner and sorceress (1640–80). From an engraving by Chasteau.

against Mme de Montespan under three heads. She had, he noted, 'attempted to get rid of Mlle de Fontanges by poison, but the evidence on that point was very doubtful'. The Princess Palatine thought otherwise. 'It is certain', she wrote, 'that La Fontanges died from poison. She herself accused La Montespan of her death. A lackey summoned by La Montespan contrived her death with powdered milk, and did away with some of her followers.' As for the second and third charges, La Reynie continued, 'she had had the sacrilegious mass celebrated on her body by [the priest] Guibourg; she had repeatedly mixed with the King's food love-philtres which were composed of cantharides, toad's dust, bat's blood, &c., deposited under the priest's chalice during mass, before they were used . . .'.

The vice-God, the man who thought himself God's regent on earth, had loved a woman who was said to have practised black magic, and to have taken part in black masses. The evidence fitted in with certain aspects of her character; the King's dizziness and headaches might now be explained by the potions she had given him. He had, some said, escaped an attempt to kill him.

Louis could not openly disgrace the mother of his legitimized children; he let her live for a few more years at Court. But their love-affair was over. The details of her conduct remained a secret in his keeping, and in 1709 he burned the relevant documents – no doubt incriminating – with his own hands.

In the 1670s the first glories of the reign disappeared. Hugues de Lionne, who had done much for foreign affairs, died in 1671, and Molière died two years later. Turenne was killed in 1675, and after that year the great Condé, weighed down with military honours, retired to Chantilly. But if the older generation was passing away, another one was taking its place. Maria Teresa had been six times a mother, but only one son, the Dauphin – *le Grand Dauphin* – survived. He was utterly indolent, and in him we may trace the origins of the indolence of Louis XV and the stupidity of Louis XVI. In 1679 the King decided that it was time for his heir to marry; and, purely on political grounds, he chose Maria of Bavaria as his son's wife. The new Dauphine soon began to live a retired life, no doubt because of her growing contempt for her husband. In due course, however, she gave birth to a son, the Duc de Bourgogne. The succession was assured. 'You will hear', wrote Mme de Sévigné, 'of the lively demonstrations of the whole Court, and with what eagerness this delight was exhibited

La Voisin and the Affair of the Poisons. This contemporary print suggests a number of her nefarious activities.

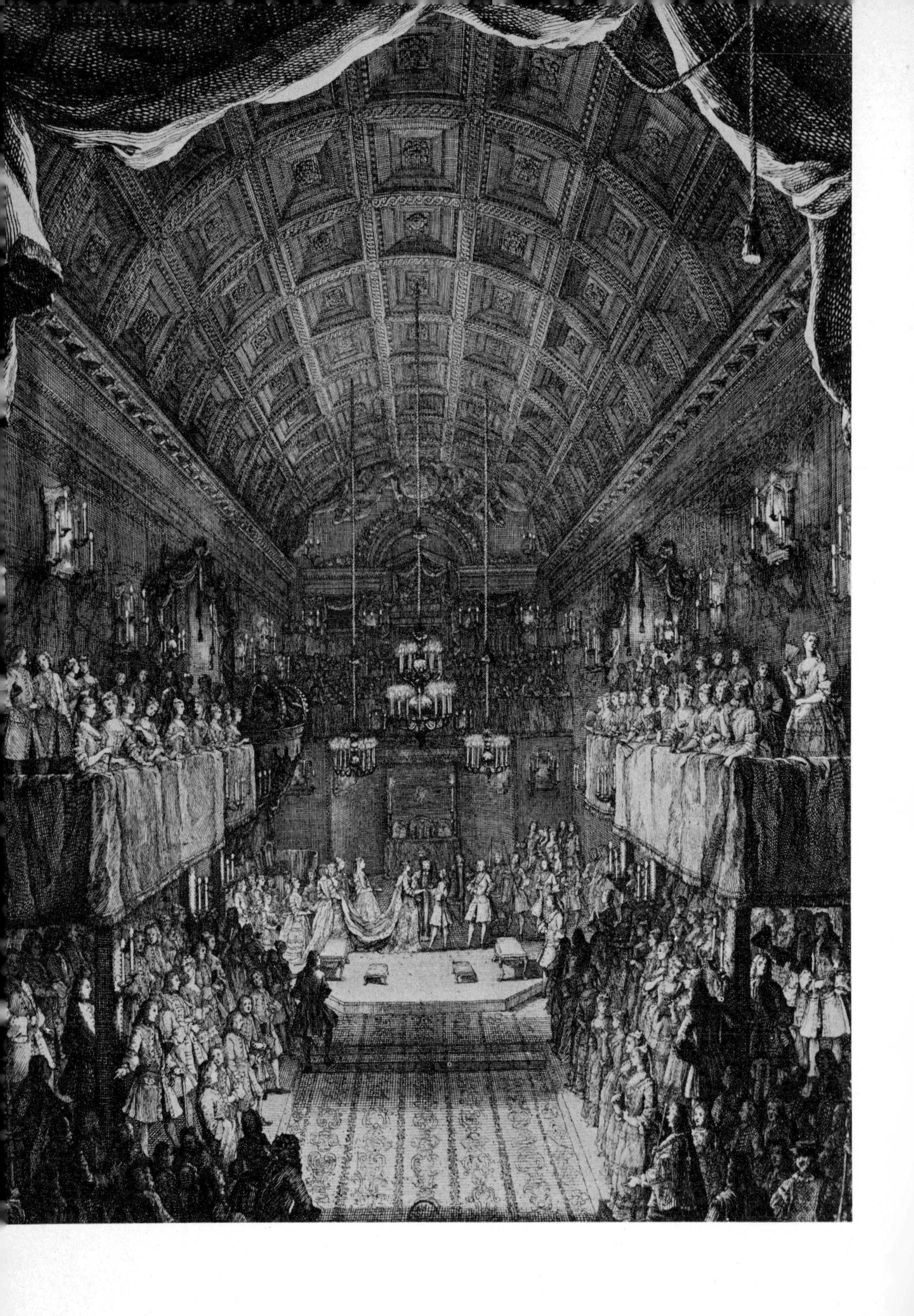

to the King, the Dauphin and the Queen; what shouts, what firing, what a pouring forth of wine, what a dance of two hundred Swiss Guards around their barrels, what cries of *Vive le Roi!*, what a ringing of all the bells in Paris. . . .' A few years later, the Dauphine bore her husband a second son, the Duc d'Anjou, and then a third, the Duc de Berri.

The year 1683, which witnessed the birth of the Duc d'Anjou, also saw the deaths of Colbert and the Queen. Perhaps the best epitaph for Maria Teresa is contained in the words of the King as he stood beside her coffin: 'Kind and forbearing friend! This is the first sorrow that you have caused me in twenty years.'

Even before the Queen had died, yet another woman had made her appearance in the King's life. She was to exercise a quite extraordinary influence upon him.

Mme Scarron – better known to posterity as Mme de Maintenon – was the grandchild of Agrippa d'Aubigné, a Huguenot leader and a friend of Henri IV. (''Tis certain', concluded an English writer, 'she is of the family of *d'Aubigny*, and not a Cook-Wench – as is commonly reported. . . . Her father was a ne'er-do-well, and she had – so legend said – been born in the prison in which he was incarcerated for debt. She spent some years in Martinique, was orphaned at the age of seven and passed from Catholicism to Protestantism and back again. At seventeen she had married Paul Scarron, the writer of burlesques. He was forty-two, immobilized and deformed by rheumatism, and in all probability the marriage was not consummated; but Françoise preferred such a marriage to the cloister. Eight years later she was left a widow; and, after a period of obscurity, she happened to meet Mme de Montespan, and became the governess of the King's children.

Was there, perhaps, a certain design in her simplicity? 'My very honoured lady,' said her spiritual adviser, 'you wear nothing but wool. But, when you kneel before me, your dress falls in such graceful folds over your feet that, somehow, I think it too perfect.' Yet if Mme Scarron was too perfect, she still employed perfection in a cause. God, she observed, 'makes use of all things to carry out His plans and to lead us slowly to the goal which we do not foresee'. The abbé mistrusted her simplicity, but the King did not. He addressed her, appropriately, as *Votre solidité*, and he showed her much respect. In the autumn of 1674 he gave her 250,000 livres to buy Maintenon, an estate near Chartres, ten miles from Versailles. It was usual for landowners to take the name of their property, and in February 1675 he addressed Mme Scarron as 'Madame de

The marriage of *le Grand Dauphin*, son of Louis XIV, and Maria of Bavaria, 7 March 1680. *Le Grand Dauphin* died in 1711; his eldest son, Louis, Duc de Bourgogne, also died before the Sun King. It was therefore the infant son of the Duc de Bourgogne who succeeded Louis XIV.

The insignia of royalty: Louis XIV invests his grandson, the infant Duc de Bourgogne, with the Order of the Holy Spirit.

The Grandsons of Louis

In 1698 when they were sixteen, fifteen and thirteen, the sons of *Le Grand Dauphin* were described thus: 'Bourgogne, a masterpiece. Delicate health. Very gay but not very chatty. Loves to study . . . Anjou, sweeter nature and also a clever boy. People prefer him to Bourgogne. Berry, very chatty, lively and full of promise.' Bourgogne caught measles from his mother and died at the age of 30. Berry had a fatal hunting accident when he was 29. Only Anjou lived into middle-age.

ABOVE The royal family relaxing at Versailles in the last decade of the seventeenth century. Since Louis XIV supported the Catholic Stuarts in England, the third child from the left is described as the Prince of Wales; he is in fact James Stuart, better known as the Old Pretender. The other two boys are the Duc d'Anjou and the Duc de Berry.

RIGHT The Duc de Berry, grandson of Louis XIV. From a pastel by Vivien at the Louvre.

ABOVE The Duc de Bourgogne, in infancy, wearing his order of chivalry.
LEFT A pawn in the politics of the Sun King: his grandson the Duc d'Anjou, who became Philip V of Spain in 1700. From a pastel by Vivien at the Louvre.

Sacred and profane love. Mlle de la Vallière and her children. From a portrait by Lely. OPPOSITE The Marquise de Montespan before her gallery at Clagny. From a portrait by an unknown artist.

Paul Scarron (1610–60), writer of burlesques, and husband of the future Mme de Maintenon.

Maintenon'. From that moment, Mme Scarron disappears from history. The King later re-created the marquisate of Maintenon in her favour, and Mme de Sévigné called her 'Madame de Maintenant'. Early in 1680 the same industrious letter-writer assured her daughter: 'Mme de Maintenon's favour increases every day; she has endless conversations with His Majesty.'

And yet 'the famous Madam de Maintenon [remained] more renown'd for her Politicks than for her Amours'. It is some measure of her character that she won the affection not only of Louis but of Maria Teresa; indeed, when the Queen was dying she took a ring from her finger, and gave it to her with the words: 'Adieu, my very dear marquise; to you I confide the happiness of the King.' Mme de Maintenon – 'the Messenger of Providence', some called her – obeyed the wishes of the dying Queen. She disliked Court life, but she was sustained by the conviction that she was responsible for the King's soul. Louis soon acquired the habit of retiring to her apartments, and listening to Racine reading one of his plays.

Even after the Queen had died, Louis's relationship with Mme de Maintenon remained platonic, for she refused to allow it to become anything else. This was, perhaps, one of the reasons why he took the final step of marriage. One night in January 1684, the Archbishop of Paris was suddenly summoned to Versailles, and there, in the presence of a handful of witnesses, the King of France and Navarre was married to the widow of Paul Scarron. Mme de Maintenon did not become Queen. She kept her own liveries, and Louis referred to her simply as 'Madame'. The marriage remained an official secret. But the secret was open. 'The Story of her Marriage to the King', observed an English critic in 1709, 'is not altogether groundless. . . . As for Children by her he had none, the Lovers (or at least she) being antiquated.'

> I can scarcely describe Mme Scarron [Louise de La Vallière had confessed]. The word prude would be applicable to her, but that is a mere shade. She is at once a bigot and a *bel esprit*. She is naturally very formal and straight-laced, but nevertheless she has been seen enacting the very humble servant of Madame de Montespan, her reader and her submissive friend. She is of a piety which appears all of a piece, alike stiff and inflexible; yet, notwithstanding, the piety has bent beneath the will of the King, and has found its joints. Madame Scarron is an admirable woman, for whom a specific term should be invented. . . . When she first appeared at Court her robe of serge, her plain linen, her black lace, exhaled such an odour of pedantry, that her very appearance gave the King the vapours. Suppleness and patience are, however, admirable qualities, which operate wonderful conversions! She now has her horses, her hôtel, and a suite of servants; she is no longer the governess of the children of Madame de Montespan, but of those of the King, which her confessor declares to be quite a different thing. This is what she has been clever enough to accomplish.

Madame de Maintenon had not merely proved to be a bewildering figure; she had aroused suspicion and dislike. And no one expressed the general mistrust and unease, the lack of sympathy that she inspired, more brilliantly than the nineteenth-century historian Jules Michelet. He described Mignard's portrait of Mme de Maintenon in the hour of her triumph:

> She is [he wrote] shrouded, revealing only what she wanted to reveal. She is magnificently gowned with coquettish prudery in rich black covered with lace (is it in mourning for the Queen?). Everything is ambiguous. She is looking and yet not looking. She holds a rose, not too rosy, slightly overblown, its semi-violet tints in harmony with the black.

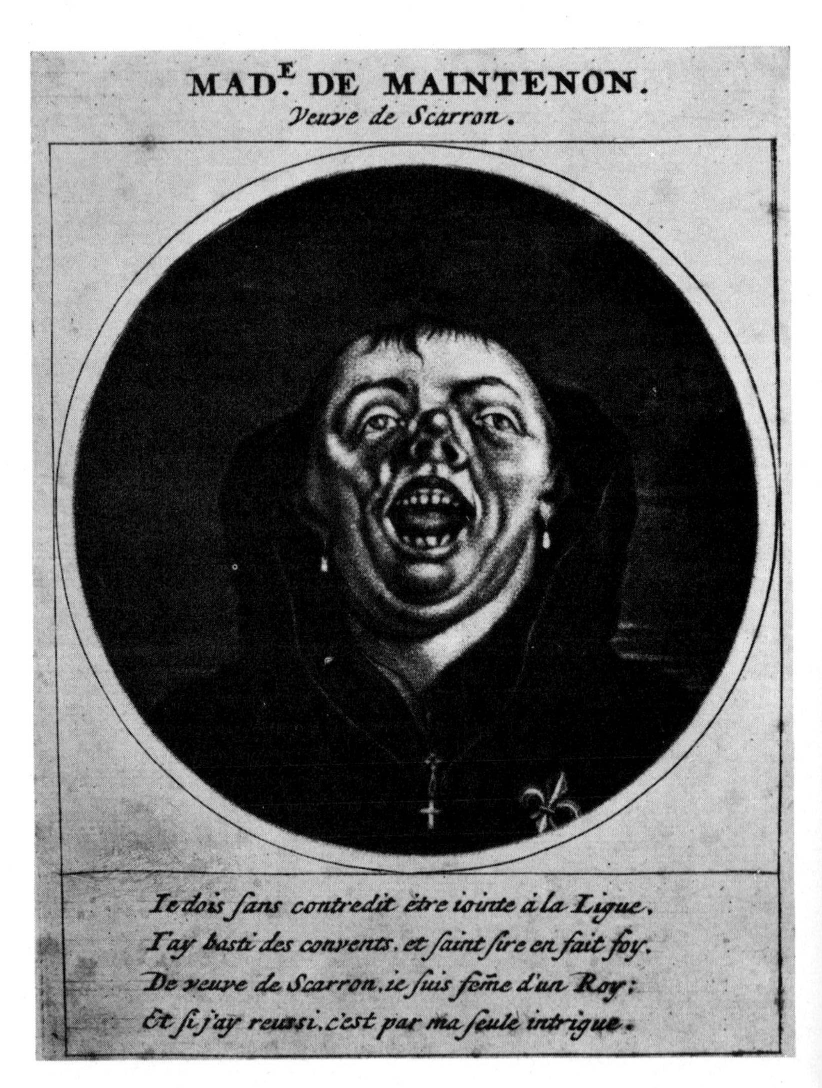

A savage caricature of Mme de Maintenon, the arch-intriguer. The verse makes it clear that her marriage to the King was an open secret.

OPPOSITE 'When you kneel before me, your dress falls in such graceful folds over your feet that, somehow, I think it too perfect.' So Mme de Maintenon was told by her spiritual adviser. This portrait of her, now at Versailles, suggests her somewhat ostentatious piety.

Madame de
Vne Dame Religieuse
qui a fait profession
Damoiselle de la
troisieme Classe
Damois
premiere
Damoiselle de l
quatrieme Class

Mme de Maintenon at Saint-Cyr. She is shown with some of the impoverished daughters of the nobility, for whom she founded the establishment.

She sits in state and governs (as a queen? a governess?). . . . Her head is quite small, but rounded and resolute. Not at all classical. In her youth she was called *la Belle Indienne,* but she must have been pretty rather than beautiful, a miniature Creole with tiny features. . . . This is not an open face. It reveals nothing of kindness, tender intimacy or equable temper. Rather, the suggestion is of a restless, active mind that will say both yes and no. There is warmth in her gaze, but it is hard, with a dry heat rarely encountered in women. Altogether, it is a twofold face. It is the portrait of *equivocation.*

The portrait is unflattering, even unpleasant. None the less, the fact remains that the King loved Mme de Maintenon, physically and mentally, longer than any woman of her age would dare to expect. Whether he loved her with his heart is another matter. No woman – except perhaps Louise de La Vallière – seems to have touched his heart since the departure of Marie Mancini. At first Mme de Maintenon showed caution and timidity; then she steadily gained confidence. She obtained what no woman before her had ever obtained. By slow degrees, she came to influence politics, without losing the attentions of an assiduous husband. All this, we are told, 'with eyes still lowered, the modesty of a nun and the authority of a moralist'.

Mme de Maintenon never imposed any strain on the treasury, and when she retired to lead the life of an abbess after the King's death, she took nothing with her. Nevertheless, she was, and remained, as unpopular as Mme de Montespan. The intolerant, hypocritical and bigoted atmosphere which she created did the King untold damage.

If Mme de Maintenon did not become Queen in marrying Louis, he did much to bring his natural children nearer the throne. He not only legitimized the children of Louise de La Vallière and Athénaïs de Montespan, he arranged marriages between them and princes and princesses of the blood. However, Mme de Maintenon's influence remained considerable. It brought an improvement in his sexual morals, and, probably as a result, the Court became extremely dull. At Versailles, the King's apartments and those of Mme de Maintenon were separated only by the Salle des Gardes; but Mme de Maintenon never appeared in public unless compelled to do so on festive occasions. In *Lettres historiques et galantes,* the correspondence between two ladies of quality, we learn that Mme de Maintenon 'never appears in public except when she goes on an outing with the King. Then she can be glimpsed at the back of the carriage, spectacles on her nose, working away at a piece of embroidery. Yet,' so one of the correspondents confessed, 'I have had the honour of speaking with her occasionally, and have found her extremely gentle and forthright. Under present circumstances, she is fearful of exciting envy. . . .' Rheumaticky, and afraid of draughts, she stayed in her rooms, and 'endeavoured to keep aloof from society, and succeeded for a time; but later on her apartment became the centre of the royal family, and to be admitted to her was everybody's ambition'.

Louis could hardly have found a woman more different from Mme de Montespan. Mme de Maintenon – like his first wife – was full of good works. Her secretary Mlle d'Aumale wrote in her memoirs that

> the sums she dispensed every year in alms were considerable. I have made up her accounts on more than one occasion. She donated between 54 and 60,000 livres a year from her income alone, without counting all the extra donations she managed to obtain from the King, the princes and all the seigneurs of the Court by dint of persuasion. In view of the added misery caused by the dreadful winter of 1709, she more than doubled her charities that year; she fed a great number of families, and maintained several convents for young girls who, without her aid, would either have died of hunger or would have been forced to beg their bread in the streets. On several occasions, when she had run out of money, she sold pieces of her furniture so that she could help some poor family whose needs had just been drawn to her attention.

Mme de Maintenon founded Saint-Cyr as an establishment for the impoverished daughters of the nobility. Mansard designed the buildings, and the King took an active interest in the scheme. When, in 1686, he first visited Saint-Cyr, he was greeted by three hundred girls singing a hymn to music by Lully. At Mme de Maintenon's request, Racine wrote *Esther* for Saint-Cyr; and early in 1689 Mme de Sévigné reported:

> The King found it admirable. Monsieur le Prince was moved to tears. Racine has never written anything more beautiful or more touching: there is a prayer of Esther's for Assuérus which carries you away. I was worried about a young girl taking the part of the King: they say that this is very good. . . . If there is a printed version of this play, it won't lie forgotten on a table.

LA DEROVTE
ET CONFVSION DES
IANSSENISTES.
la Religion
le Pape
la Puissa
la Concorde
le Roy
la Pieté
le Iansenisme
la Tromperie
la Iustice
LE PAPE
Puis que du St. Esprit l'Eglise Illuminée
D'vne fausse doctrine accuse les autheurs
Par la puissance enfin q. Dieu no.s a donnée
Nous Condamno.s leurs secte et to.s le.rs Sectate.s
LE ROY
Poussé par la Concorde envuz d'un Divin
Qui maintient nos Sujets dans lesprit d
Prestons po.r abollir vne Erreur Crimine
Le bras de la justice a la Religion.

7 The Years of Decline

THE RELIGIOUS VEIN HAD NEVER BEEN WANTING in Louis's character, and his confessor had always had an influence on his behaviour. But under Mme de Maintenon the whole tone of the Court had changed. The splendid gaiety of the early years was thrown aside, and piety came into fashion at Versailles. Unfortunately, Louis's piety became excessive and misdirected: he determined to ensure the existence of a wholly Catholic France. He turned against the Protestants (or Huguenots); and in 1681 Mme de Maintenon wrote happily: 'If God preserve the King there will not be one Huguenot left twenty years hence.' In 1680 he had begun to send missionaries into strongly Huguenot areas; at the same time he decreed that Huguenots must not hold certain public offices. Huguenot churches were razed to the ground.

The King [explained the Abbé de Choisy] began to think of directing his zeal towards the banishment of heresy from his States. This had always occupied his mind since he assumed power, and the grand design had gradually formed itself in his mind. The Chambers set up by the Edict of Nantes had all been suppressed. More than four hundred temples had been destroyed; the Huguenots were no longer allowed to hold posts in the police forces or departments of finance; farming was barred to them; no physicians or midwives might be members of their faith; it was even becoming difficult for them to achieve advancement in a military career. These restrictions were both reasonable and wise, but they did not seem vigorous enough to a zealous and powerful King who imagined that he would attain divine glory if he was prepared to sacrifice to politics in this most important matter. In this he was encouraged by Louvois.

Many middle-class Huguenots, satisfied with their freedom of worship, had devoted themselves to industry with notable success. But now, impelled by his passion for uniformity, Louis issued edicts closing Huguenot churches and schools. There were mass conversions to Catholicism – conversions achieved by force, and not by faith. Nicolas-Joseph Foucault, *intendant* of the Pau region, wrote in his memoirs:

PREVIOUS PAGES Louis XIV determines to abolish 'a criminal error': the existence of Jansenism. This contemporary engraving, 'The Rout and Confusion of the Jansenists', illustrates the religious persecution which characterized the later years of the reign.

On 18 April 1685, I asked M. de Louvois for blank warrants which would allow me to billet one or more companies in the towns where these religionists are strongly established, since I felt sure that the mere approach of the troops would produce a great number of conversions. I assured him that I would exercise strict control over the soldiers to see that they did no violence, and said I would accept responsibility for any complaints he might receive. . . . M. de Louvois having sent me several blank warrants, six hundred people in five towns and villages were immediately converted on hearing the news that the companies were on the march.

By the autumn of 1685, the Huguenots had been reduced by three-quarters; most of them had become Catholics, others had infringed the law and been sent to the galleys. Some had emigrated; but when numbers of the most industrious artisans began to leave the country, Louis forbade emigration. Those Huguenots who still remained were protected by the Edict of Nantes, by which Henri IV had recognized Protestantism, and had guaranteed their religious freedom. This edict contradicted Louis's notion of unity, and on 18 October 1685 he revoked it.

Saint-Simon described the Revocation as

> the appalling conspiracy that depopulated a quarter of the realm, weakened it in every part, subjected it for a long while to open, admitted pillage by the dragoons, authorized the tortures that led thousands of men and women to their deaths, ruined a great community, tore countless families apart, armed relative against relative, . . . made a gift of our manufactures to foreign nations, . . . and gave them the spectacle of a prodigious number of people outlawed, stripped, fleeing, vagrant though guiltless of crime, seeking asylum far from their native land.

The Huguenots who lived in the wild part of the country between Gard and Lozère broke out in the terrible revolt of the Camisards. Louis was forced to attack his own subjects. In the cause of religion, he had lost more than he could have gained by the most victorious war, more than his enemies would have asked as the price of the most disastrous peace. Many Huguenots escaped and carried their thrift and skill to the enemies of France. Holland dates its industrial revival and Brandenburg its industrial life from 1685. It is said that over 400,000 inhabitants were lost to France by Louis's persecution. The Huguenots did not regain legal standing in France until 1801.

The Revocation was an unforgivable act of interference in the spiritual affairs of other men. It was also the act of an absolute monarch, and Bossuet, always a courtier, exhorted his flock from his pulpit: 'Let us spread the news of this modern miracle, let us pour out our hearts on the piety of Louis; let us . . . tell this new Constantine, this new Theodosius, this new Marcian, this new Charlemagne: "What you have done is worthy of your reign. It gives it its true stamp. Through you heresy is no more; God alone has performed this wonderful thing."'

But Louis had not revoked the Edict of Nantes as an act of piety; he had done so to increase his own glory. As the reign continued, he was more and more often led astray by his love of *la gloire.* Even in diplomacy and war, which were the essential *métier de roi,* he outlived his skill and good fortune. The success of France under Richelieu and Mazarin had been founded on *la modération dans la force,* the classic French foreign policy. Louis XIV pushed his ambitions to the point at which they caused the creation of a hostile coalition powerful enough to defeat France itself.

The King in Council: an engraving by Jan Luiken of the Revocation of the Edict of Nantes (1685). Like Louis's attack on the Jansenists, his persecution of the Huguenots was an unforgivable act of interference in the spiritual affairs of other men.

His gains at Nijmegen had led him to believe that nothing could check French expansion in the East. When the Elector of the Palatinate died childless in 1685, Louis laid claim to the country which lies north of Alsace on the French side of the Rhine. His claim was so ludicrous that one surmises megalomania. He claimed the Palatinate because the Elector's sister was Monsieur's second wife, and therefore his own sister-in-law. Europe was amazed and alarmed, and in 1686 William of Orange formed the League of Augsburg against him. The League consisted of Spain, the Empire, Sweden and various German princes. When Louis invaded the Palatinate in 1688, the League declared war against him; in 1689 it was joined by England, who that year proclaimed William as her new King. The War of the League of Augsburg was to last until 1697. For the second time in his reign, as the result of an act of aggression, Louis found himself obliged, virtually single-handed, to fight a long war against the leading powers of Europe.

The third and last phase of his reign began in 1689, with the formation of the Grand Alliance against him, and it shows a steady decline in his powers. Not content with the long and quite unnecessary war in the Palatinate, Louis supported the Catholic James II, now in exile, in his attempt to regain the English throne. In 1690 James set off for Ireland with a French fleet. The Battle of the Boyne ended the hopes of a Stuart restoration, and James returned to France, where Louis continued to place Saint-Germain at his disposal, and gave him an annual pension of £200,000.

In Louis's policy we may trace the pernicious influence of Louvois. The son of Michel Le Tellier, he had shared the Ministry of War with his father from 1662 to about 1677, after which he occupied the position of Minister alone. A remarkable administrator, he had reorganized the French army; but he had instigated religious persecution, and he had encouraged the King's inclination for war. He had been largely responsible for Louis's devastation of the Palatinate. In 1691, on the death of Louvois, Louis became his own Minister of War. 'Idleness', as Visconti said, 'never knew so redoubtable a foe.' He worked for eight or nine hours a day, and often held a morning and afternoon council. In 1691 he was present at the capture of Mons, and the following spring he decided that he himself would direct the siege of Namur, one of the strongest Spanish fortresses in the Netherlands. It was his last personal success in battle, for after 1693 when he was after all 55,

he left command in the field to his generals.

His achievements were not universally admired. In 1690, the author of *The Most Christian Turk* gave his view of 'the Life and Bloody Reign of Lewis XIV'. He declared his detestation of 'that Prince, who has for many years . . . made such a noise and bluster in the World, to the damage and disturbance of all Christendom, and has, as it were, fattened himself with Christian blood'. English criticism might be expected. But in the closing years of his life, Louis was harshly criticized even in France. 'What stung the King', Saint-Simon wrote, 'was the torrent of exceedingly bold and immoderate lampoons against his person, his conduct, and his rule, that were to be found for some time posted at the gates of Paris, in churches, in public places, and especially on statues of him, which were defaced by night. . . . There was also a multitude of verses and songs in which nothing was spared.' A threatening

OPPOSITE In 1686 William of Orange formed the League of Augsburg to check the territorial ambitions of Louis XIV. When Louis invaded the Palatinate in 1688 the League declared war against him; in 1689 it was joined by England, who that year proclaimed William as her new King. William III – as he became – was one of the most consistent opponents of *le Roi Soleil*. In this portrait – attributed to J. Wyck – he is seen in armour, with a battle scene in the background.

On 8 April 1691, during the War of the League of Augsburg, Louis XIV was present at the capture of Mons. This engraving shows him in the trenches with his brother, Monsieur (left foreground), the Duc de Bourbon and the Duc de Chartres.

underground pamphlet was passed from hand to hand, which recited the litany: 'Our hallowed father, which art in Versailles . . .'.

As the glory of Louis XIV passed under heavy clouds, he became more intolerant; but criticism made itself heard. Fénelon had been tutor to the Duc de Bourgogne, and his *Télémaque* reveals the ideas which he had tried to inspire in his pupil. All Fénelon's writings imply a criticism of the absolutist system of Louis XIV; but the most hostile judgment is found in a letter which he wrote to the King, probably in 1691. The fate of the letter is mysterious, and it is unlikely that so bitter an indictment ever reached the eyes of the King himself. In this letter, Fénelon denounced the Dutch war as the source of all the others; he derided the King's military preparations, and directly attacked his ideals and his character. 'You are praised to the skies', he wrote, 'for having impoverished France, and you have built your throne on the ruin of all classes in the State.'

Fénelon spoke with feeling. In the last decade of the seventeenth century, and the first years of the century that followed, the King continued his religious persecution. Jansenism was the doctrine drawn by Cornelius Jansen, a former Bishop of Ypres, from the works of St Augustine. It was a doctrine which approximated to Calvinism, repudiated the effectiveness of the human will and asserted predestination and the sole virtue of divine grace as against the doctrine of salvation by works. The strength of Jansenism lay in its moral austerity, which influenced many people who did not accept its doctrines. By the end of the seventeenth century, this influence permeated the Court, society and literature of France; and it has been said that, of the great writers of the period, only Molière and La Fontaine escaped it. Its most famous exponent was Pascal. Jansenism was strongly opposed by the Jesuits; and, in the last years of his reign, under Jesuit influence, Louis took the final steps to have Jansenism condemned among his subjects. In 1705 he obtained a Bull from Clement XI, and Jansenist doctrine was proclaimed heretical. On Louis's orders the abbey of Port-Royal, where the doctrine was chiefly practised, was razed to the ground.

There was another school of religious thought with which he came into conflict, and this was Quietism. If the Jansenists were the Calvinists of Roman Catholicism, the Quietists were the Quakers. Their fundamental tenet was that final union with God is reached when the soul is in a state of perfect inaction, and that in this union the soul is purely passive under the action of the

OPPOSITE The defeat of the French fleet at La Hogue, May 1692, by the combined English and Dutch fleets under Edward Russell, first Earl of Orford.

A TRUE DRAUGHT & PROSPECT OF THE LATE ENGAGEMENT
between yᵉ English & yᵉ French FLEETS on yᵉ 19/29 May 1692: at 6½ Leag. in yᵉ NE of Cap Barfleur
Coast of Havre de grace
St Mark
Bay of la Hogue
Carentan
King James Camp
Cap Barfleur
IST OF THE FRENCH SHIPS
urnt at Cherbourg & la Hogue.
The Royal Sun (French Adm.) of ... 110. guns
The Ambitious ... 102.
The Marveilleux, or Wonderfull ... 96.
The Admirable ... 90.
The Foudroyant, or Thunderstriking 90.
The Magnifique, or Stately ... 80.
The S. Philipe ... 80.
The Thundering ... 74.
The Terrible ... 74.
The Bourbon ... 64.

The Grand Dauphin with his wife and sons. The Duc de Bourgogne is in red, the Duc d'Anjou is in blue and the Duc de Berry is in white. From a painting by Pierre Mignard.

'This, Sir, is the Duc d'Anjou, whom you may salute as your king.' Louis XIV presents his grandson to the Spanish Ambassador at Versailles, 16 November 1700. This latest example of the King's *folie de grandeur* led to the Grand Alliance of 1701 and to the ten-year War of the Spanish Succession.

Divine Light. Perfect inaction held no appeal for Louis.

Fénelon had been drawn to Quietism. He was a man of great ability, but – so it is said – of greater ambition, and he probably hoped to play the part of Richelieu and Mazarin when his pupil the Duc de Bourgogne succeeded to the throne. However, when he published his *Explication des Maximes des Saints*, the Pope was persuaded to condemn it. Louis himself had written to Innocent XII that ecclesiastical readers had found the book 'very bad and very dangerous'; he had urged the Pope to take action, and he was overjoyed when he did so. Where religion was concerned, Louis appeared at his worst.

France was disturbed by religious persecution. In politics and warfare, one disaster followed another. In 1692 the French fleet was defeated at La Hogue. France was obliged to renounce the Low Countries and the Spanish inheritance. In 1697, at the Treaty of Ryswick, which ended the War of the League of Augsburg, Louis, the supporter of James II, was obliged to recognize William III, the Protestant 'usurper', as King of Great Britain and Ireland.

The age of distinguished and dominant statesmen was over. From 1700 to 1713, the King surrounded himself with minions who could only do his will. He was growing old, and his mind was rigidly set; he refused to learn that the days of absolute monarchy were ending, that his ambitions of conquest must be restrained. In November 1700 he accepted the Spanish Succession for the Duc d'Anjou, who also maintained his rights to the French throne. On 16 November he summoned the Spanish Ambassador to an audience at Versailles, and there he presented his grandson to the diplomat, with the words: 'This, Sir, is the Duc d'Anjou, whom you may salute as your king.'

Even at Versailles, there were some who felt that the King had gone too far. A correspondent from Court confessed:

> Everybody here expects a terrible war to break out next spring, and preparations are already being made for this eventuality. So now the kingdom is going to be ruined once again, before it has had time even to make good the ravages of the last war. Frankly, I think that we are going to pay dearly for this crown of Spain which the King has bought for his grandson at our expense. It will cost us a fortune to prevent it being snatched away from him. Frankly, we are great fools to ruin ourselves for the aggrandizement of others, and, moreover, for people who, far from doing us honour and being grateful to us, regard us as a worthless servant of the Gospel who does not perform his allotted tasks– but I say no more for fear that I have already said too much.

The correspondent's fears were justified. Louis's action led to the Grand Alliance of 1701: the coalition of Catholic Austria and the Protestant maritime nations. The War of the Spanish Succession began, and it lasted for ten years; it brought notable defeats at Cremona, Ramillies and Oudenarde. France was in economic and financial chaos, she was nearing the end of her resources, and the King was obliged to have recourse to the financiers. He found relaxation only in his new retreat, his château at Marly.

He needed relaxation. He was seventy-five when the latest war came to an end. He had to fight on every side: against the Protestants in the Cévennes, against the poverty which followed the Great Winter of 1709. Saint-Simon reported that the winter was worse than any within living memory. 'A bitter frost continued without respite for two months, freezing the rivers down to their very mouths and making the edge of the sea so hard that heavily laden waggons were driven over it.' 'I have never in my life seen such miserable times', wrote the Princess Palatine, from

Versailles, on 2 March 1709. 'The people are dying of the cold like flies. The windmill sails are frozen in their sockets, no corn can be ground, and many people are dying of starvation.' Mme de Maintenon, pious as ever, enquired of the Princesse des Ursins:

How can you say, Madame, that God is not declaring Himself against us, when He sends us a winter unparalleled for a hundred and five or six years, . . . which not only spares not a single fruit for the present, but freezes all the trees? The olive trees in Provence and Languedoc, the chestnuts in Limousin and the walnut trees all over France are ruined for years to come. We see the poor dying of hunger, but we cannot succour them because our lands no longer yield!

Spanish pride and French luxury. In this French cartoon, which appeared at the time of the War of the Spanish Succession, the Spaniards ridicule the vanity of the French, and assure them that war will teach them wisdom.

The King was faced not only with misery at home, but with the threat of invasion in the north. He had to fight a bitter and more personal battle against death. It took his son, the Grand Dauphin, in 1711, and in 1712 it took his grandson, the Duc de Bourgogne; the young man of whom Fénelon had hoped to make a liberal and virtuous king, a peace-loving sovereign, in a reinvigorated nation. The long War of the Spanish Succession ended with the Peace of Utrecht in 1713. France kept its territorial integrity, but Spain remained the kingdom of Philip V, and England won important maritime concessions.

Failure and disaster did not weaken the resolution of the ageing monarch. In the midst of defeat and discontent, the King stood unshaken. His physique remained magnificent, his confidence in divine sanction and in his kingly duty remained supreme. And yet it is clear that he felt the misfortunes of France; and Mme de Maintenon recorded that he often came into her room, and locked the door, and that sometimes he shed uncontrollable tears. On occasion he showed an unexpected glimpse of his humanity; but in his final years the firmness of his character upheld him still. Absolutism and bureaucracy kept France in a frozen grip, apparently immobile. Underneath, new currents were stirring, but they were only to appear on the surface in a new reign.

But the age was weary of the long and now disastrous reign of Louis XIV. France was ready for his death. It was long and painful. By June 1715 it was – as he knew – already the subject of speculation. On 18 June he remarked during supper: 'If I go on eating with as good an appetite as I do at present, I shall be the ruin of a whole host of Englishmen who have wagered huge sums that I will die before the first of September.'

At the beginning of August, he received the ambassador of the King of Persia. He 'put on a costume made from a black and gold material encrusted with diamonds to the tune of more than 12,500,000 livres, and the costume was so heavy that he changed out of it immediately after dinner'. He was not only old and weary. On 11 August he began to have pain in his leg. It was diagnosed as sciatica, and he was carried about in a chair. On about 24 August, the King's chief surgeon saw black spots on the

What good can you Expect for all your pains
When We are drove in Wooden Shooes & Chains
Oh Maintenon Oh Lewis wheres your Brains

leg, and recognized gangrene. The King was made to keep his leg in a bath of Burgundy, and he was prescribed asses' milk. It was too late for amputation. He was in constant pain.

Popular art of the early eighteenth century: a playing card which refers to the War of the Spanish Succession.

Louis was serenely aware that he was dying; and, ever conscious of his rôle, he had made arrangements for his funeral. Now that the fifth and final act of his life had arrived, he played his part with proper ceremonial. He summoned his dignitaries and servants, and bade farewell to them:

> Gentlemen, I ask forgiveness for the bad example I have set you. You have served me loyally and with a desire to please me. It vexes me not to have rewarded you better. Bad times are the cause. I ask on my grandson's behalf for the same application and the same loyalty that you have shown to me. He is a child who may have many setbacks. . . . Follow the orders that my nephew [the Regent] will give you, *he is to rule the realm*. I hope that he will do it well. I also hope that you will all contribute towards unity, and that if anybody strays you will rescue him. I feel that I am becoming emotional and that I am making you emotional too. I ask your pardon. Farewell, gentlemen, I rely on you to remember me sometimes.

The royal family were summoned, no doubt in order of precedence. The last to be sent for was the King's great-grandson, the five-year-old son of the Duc de Bourgogne. The Dauphin was brought in by his governess, Mme de Ventadour.

> My dear child [said Louis XIV], you are going to be a great king. Do not copy me in my love of building or my love of warfare. On the contrary, try to live peacefully with your neighbours. Remember your duty and your obligations to God; see that your subjects honour Him. Take good advice and follow it, try to improve the lot of your people as I, unfortunately, have never been able to do. Do not forget what you owe to Mme de Ventadour. Madame, I should like to kiss him.

He kissed the child; and, as he did so, he said: 'My dear child, I give you my blessing with all my heart.' From now on it was noticed that he spoke of the little boy as the King and of himself as already gone: 'In the days when I was King.' He added: 'I depart. France remains.'

27 August and the morning of the 28th were devoted to his wife. Mme de Maintenon, with her secretary, Mlle d'Aumale, remained alone with him. They burned sheafs of papers, among them Mme de Maintenon's letters to Louis. He asked her to burn the letters which he himself had written her. Almost nothing

Louis XIV died on 1 September 1715. Here he lies in state at Saint-Denis on 9 September.

survives of this correspondence; if we possessed it, much of history might have to be rewritten.

On the afternoon of the 30th, with Racinian control, the King said to Mme de Maintenon: 'Do not wait any longer, Madame, it is a sorry spectacle. I hope that it will soon be at an end.' Françoise consulted her confessor. He looked at the dying man, and assured her: 'He no longer needs you.' She went to her apartment and shared out the furniture among her servants. At five o'clock she left Versailles. That evening, the courtiers also made their departure, and left the King to the chaplains, the

physicians and the *valets de chambre*. The Duc du Maine, the King's son by Mme de Montespan, was giving a celebration supper.

Louis XIV died at a quarter past eight on the morning of Sunday, 1 September 1715, just three days before his seventy-seventh birthday, in the seventy-second year of his reign. He atoned for the adulation of a lifetime. As his body was taken to the basilica of Saint-Denis, it was escorted by a brawling, drunken mob, howling with joy. The *canaille*, whom he had despised, at last made their comment on him.

8
The Century of Louis XIV

Jansenism had its headquarters in two convents, Port-Royal in Paris and Port-Royal-des-Champs, shown here, which was near Versailles. Courtiers would often visit relations there. When Mme de Maintenon said that she would help Racine back into favour he replied, 'You never will, for my aunt at Port-Royal, who is more important with God than you are with the King is praying night and day that I should be chastened.' Sadly he was right. Nor did the convent fare better. The inhabitants were dispersed by Louis in 1709 and the buildings destroyed the following year. From paintings by an unknown artist.

PREVIOUS PAGES Detail of an urn in the gardens of Versailles. Surrounded by sun-rays and branches of laurel, this head of Apollo recalls the triumphs of *le Roi Soleil*.

ONCE AGAIN THERE WAS A REGENCY: this time for Louis XV. The new sovereign had his predecessor's last words inscribed on vellum, and it is said that he carried them with him for the rest of his life. Mme de Maintenon retired to Saint-Cyr. 'I saw the King die like a hero and a saint', she said. 'I have exchanged the world, for which I never cared, for the loveliest retreat I ever desired.' She died there, some four years later, on 15 April 1719. She was eighty-four.

'Did you think, then, that I was immortal?' Louis XIV had enquired of his weeping valets, as he lay dying. They had indeed. He had had the longest reign recorded in history. Yet his reign had ended in disaster, and already, in 1709, an English critic had declared: 'We shall not find him so great a Man as the World has believed him to be.' Saint-Simon, who had known his Court, had no doubt of his greatest failing: 'He acquired a pride so colossal that, truly, had not God implanted in his heart the fear of the devil, even in his worst excesses, he would literally have allowed himself to be worshipped. . . . From this false pride stemmed all that ruined him. We have already seen some of its ill-effects. Others are yet to come.' Voltaire agreed with Saint-Simon; in 1751, in *Le Siècle de Louis XIV*, he concluded: 'This monarch loved grandeur and glory in everything. If a prince had done such great things as he did, and was also simple and modest, he would be the first of Kings, and Louis XIV the second.'

Louis XIV was endowed with some truly regal qualities. Above all, he knew how to choose the chief agents of his policy at home and abroad. But he himself was no great statesman and nothing of a general. He lacked the genius of Napoleon. His monarchy was not his creation – as the Empire was to be that of Bonaparte. On the other hand, the system of absolute government, which he carried on for more than half a century, was characteristic of the age of which he was the most conspicuous figure. Montesquieu decided that Louis's character was more remarkable than his intelligence. It was a fair judgment on *le Grand Monarque*.

Ernest Lavisse, the republican historian, left a portrait of him which remains unequalled. Louis, he said, had good looks, vigour, grace, a love of his calling, a noble idea of professional duty, and diligence in its performance. His intellectual education had been virtually non-existent, his political education inadequate and corrupting. Above all, he had inherited pride, a cult – or passion – for glory, and this inheritance weighed upon a man who was, when all was said, an ordinary human being. There was always

a danger that egoism might become self-worship, that devotion to duty might turn towards the satisfaction of mere vanity. Louis XIV deserved to be called the Great King; but it was remarkable that no one had ever called him a great man. He was great as the officiant of royalty; he wore the greatness of France as if it were his proper dress. He was the very type of the personage known as a king. He was a document and a brilliant witness in the history of monarchical power, which is also that of the astonishing aptitude of man for admiration and obedience. But, stripped of his royalty, he was a gentleman, an *honnête homme*, like many another contemporary at Court or in Paris.

'The King is dead: Long live the King!' On the day of Louis XIV's death, the five-year-old Louis XV, attended by the Regent, the Duc d'Orléans (left), receives the homage of the Cardinal de Noailles.

No sovereign in French history seems more remote than Louis XIV from the people whom he ruled. Louis XIV was the embodiment of the State, a demi-god, but he had disdained, mistakenly, to be a human being. He had done everything to ensure his glory, and the glory of the nation, except what – to modern thinking – matters most. He had not ensured the welfare of his people. He had

moved in an artificial world, largely of his own creation, and he had ignored the great mass of his subjects. He was engrossed in the ritual of Versailles. He did not understand life as it was lived by the *petits bourgeois*, the farmers and the peasants of France.

'There are certain fierce animals, male and female, scattered through the country, livid, swarthy, scorched by the sun, attached to the earth which they dig and shift with invincible stubbornness. They have a kind of articulate voice, and, when they rise to their feet, they show a human face – and in fact they are human. . . .': La Bruyère saw the French peasantry, noted them and passed on. He was not concerned with curing the evils of society. Nor, alas, was his sovereign. To Louis XIV the vast majority of Frenchmen existed only as tillers of the soil, payers of taxes and material for his armies. He showed no interest or care, let alone compassion, for most of his subjects. They were, at times, the objects of his reforming zeal; they were not accorded Christian charity. Socially and humanly speaking, they did not exist for him. Perhaps it would be more true to say that, after the Fronde, he was afraid of the power of the people. His concern was simply to repress it.

Perhaps one cannot blame him for failing to show the liberal and humanitarian instincts of later ages. At least he took his profession and his religion seriously. He was splendidly conscientious, but his so-called *Mémoires* do not show the breadth of vision, the bold generalizations about the art of government that we find in the writings of Napoleon. Louis's intense application had its weaknesses; he never allowed himself to unbend. Unremittingly he played a part. Thackeray drew an all too eloquent caricature of *le Roi Soleil*: he contrasted the monarch in periwig and robes with the bald, obese man inside them.

But France was not Louis XIV; it was not the Court, that narrow circle which would have liked to ignore the rest of the world. The real France was represented by her soldiers and her sailors, by the prosperous bourgeoisie, drawn by Molière. It was represented by Molière himself and Racine, by Le Brun and Le Nôtre, by Mansard and Lully, by diligent administrators and diplomats, by Colbert, by the peasants and craftsmen, the backbone of the nation. The greatness of France lay in men like these, and Versailles was only a symbol of transient glory.

Louis XIV – like his distant successor General de Gaulle – was finally led astray by his dream, destroyed by his *folie de grandeur*. Rigid, old and absolute, he lost sight of the currents of politics,

The Grand Monarch: Louis XIV on horseback, from a painting by Van der Meulen.

he was blind to the realities of power. Absolute monarchy may last as long as the monarch himself; but it demands a great man to sustain it. Louis XIV outlived his 'genius' by many years. Long before he died, he had brought monarchy into discredit. He had also failed – though he thought himself to be supremely wise – to recognize the beginning of a more democratic age. If he had condescended to adapt himself, if, above all, he had gained the love of his people, he might have left a more secure throne to his successor. As it was, the dissipations of the Regent, the weakness of Louis XV, the stupidity of Louis XVI, merely worsened the damage he had done. The Bourbons were never to understand the art of monarchy in modern times. The Revolution was to teach them nothing. In the nineteenth century, during the Bourbon Restoration, Louis XVIII and Charles X still attempted autocratic rule. Their attempt duly ended with the Revolution of 1830.

Louis XIV had had the stature to play the absolute monarch. He had had a grandeur of conception. He was a titanic figure, almost a force of nature. The mere length of his reign, the power of his energy, the size of his appetites, the extent of his ambitions: all of them were greater than those of his contemporaries. He was not only an imposing man, he was a consummate actor, and he understood how to play his part. Louis XIV loved power as an artist does. After him, every national leader had to be a man of the theatre.

His weaknesses were quite as impressive as his virtues. He was a poor husband to his official wife. He was led into dangerous paths by Mme de Montespan – and her influence lasted for many years. Mme de Maintenon's piety led him far astray. His religious persecution was indefensible. He did little, it appears, to end the barbarous customs of his time: the tortures which were carried out in the name of the law. He was responsible for untold oppression and cruelty.

At times, in his affection for his mother, his love for Marie Mancini, we feel that the King had endearing qualities. He could, at times, act from the heart, not from the head. Yet, when all is said, he was not an endearing figure. He inspires a sense of wonder, but no affection. He allows us to see the personage of the King; but we often wonder if there is a heart or soul inside. We marvel at the vast, protracted creation of Versailles; but we remember the many workmen who died in building it, and the treasuries of money spent on glory while La Bruyère's brutish peasants laboured on.

Louis XIV at sixty-one. A contemporary engraving.

He had been, in many ways, a disastrous king; but, three-quarters of a century after his death, the disasters of his reign were to precipitate France into modern times. The French Revolution marked the beginning of democracy on the Continent of Europe. Michelet remarked that the age of Louis XIV ended everything and initiated nothing. One might say, perhaps, that it ended the old order in most of Europe; it initiated a movement, of gathering momentum, towards liberal ideas and democratic rule. In 1714, the year before Louis's death, George I ascended the English throne. The Hanoverian dynasty, for all its failings, was to show the cardinal merit which Louis XIV had despised: the merit of a constitutional monarchy, increasingly aware of the nation's will. A monarchy cannot survive on grandeur alone: it ultimately depends on the will of the people. It gains strength from their prosperity, admiration and affection.

And yet, as Voltaire said, whatever people have written against him, no one will mention Louis XIV without respect, and without recalling a memorable century. The literature of his time has always been considered by the French themselves as most thoroughly representative of the culture to which it belongs. People, too, will always speak of *le style Louis XIV*; and they will see it symbolized in the palace which the King created and continued to transform for half a century. Louis XIV had determined that Versailles should be one of the noblest places on earth; and Le Nôtre, with inspiration, had used the landscape to prolong the theatre of majesty into the illimitable distance.

A triumphal arch erected in honour of Louis XIV, at the end of the Faubourg Saint-Antoine, in Paris. Designed by Claude Perrault, and built of plaster, at the city's expense, it was set up in 1670, and demolished in 1716, the year after Louis's death. *Sic transit gloria mundi.*

Further Reading

Ashley, Maurice, *Louis XIV and the Greatness of France* (Free Press, New York, 1965)

Barnwell, H. T. (translated and edited), *Selected Letters of Madame de Sévigné* (Dent, London, 1960)

Blennerhassett, Charlotte, *Louis XIV and Madame de Maintenon* (George Allen and Sons, London, 1910)

Church, William F., *The Greatness of Louis XIV – Myth or Reality?* (D.L.Heath and Co., Boston, 1959)

Cole, Charles W., *Colbert and a Century of French Mercantalism* (2 volumes, Columbia University Press, New York, 1939)

Cronin, Vincent, *Louis XIV* (The Reprint Society, London, 1965)

Dyson, C.C., *Madame de Maintenon, Her Life and Times* (John Lane, London, New York, 1909)

Erlanger, Philippe, *Louis XIV* translated by Stephen Cox (Weidenfeld and Nicolson, London 1970)

Haldane, Charlotte, *Madame de Maintenon, Uncrowned Queen of France* (Constable, London, 1970)

Hassall, A., *Mazarin* (London, 1896)

Lair, Jules Auguste, *Louise de la Vallière and the Early Life of Louis XIV* (New York, 1908)

Petrie, Sir Charles, *Louis XIV* (Thornton Butterworth, London, 1938)

Sutherland, Monica, *Louis XIV and Marie Mancini* (Jonathan Cape, London, 1956)

Williams, Hugh Noel, *Madame de Montespan and Louis XIV* (Harper and Bros, London and New York, 1939)

Family tree of Louis XIV

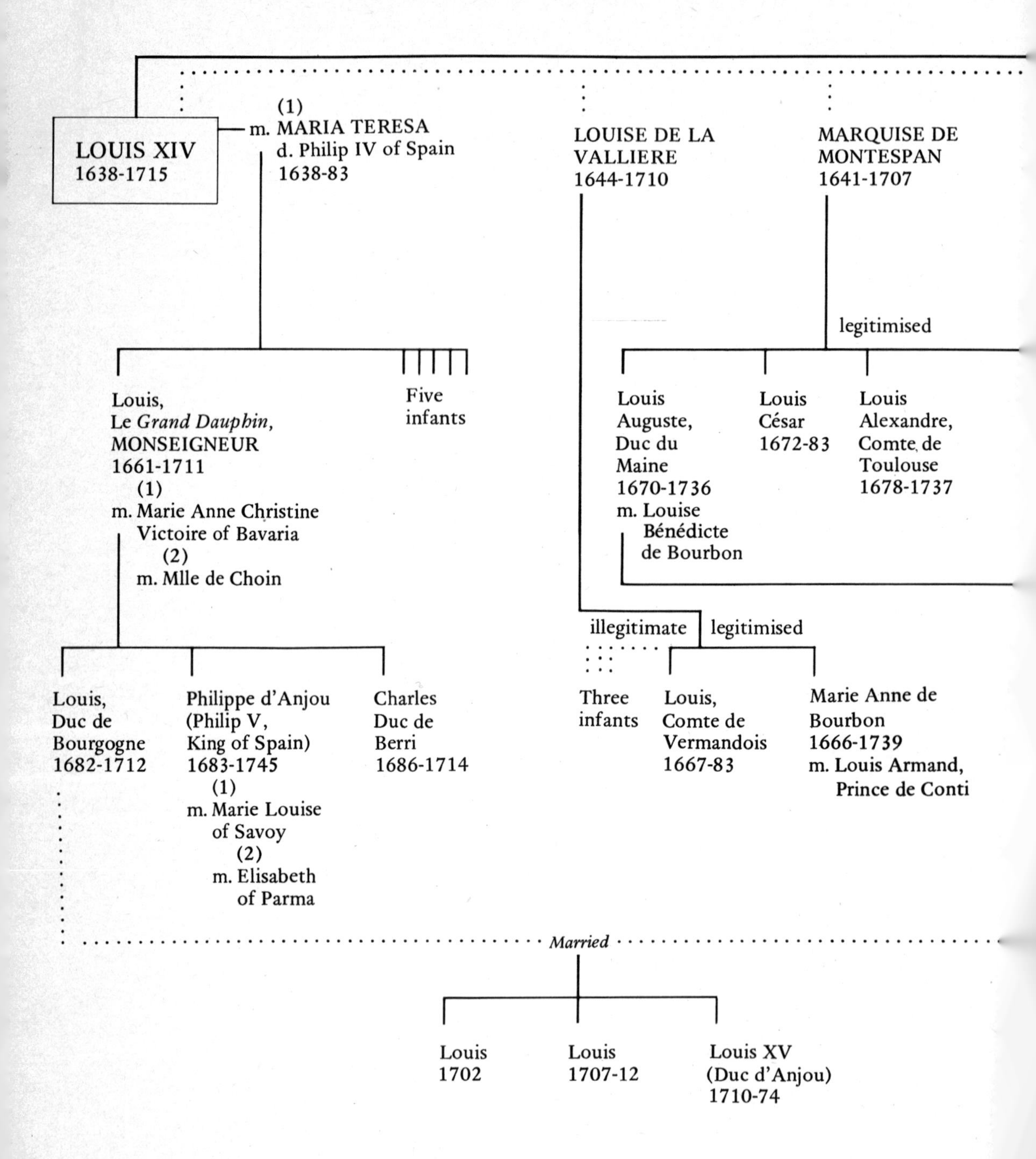

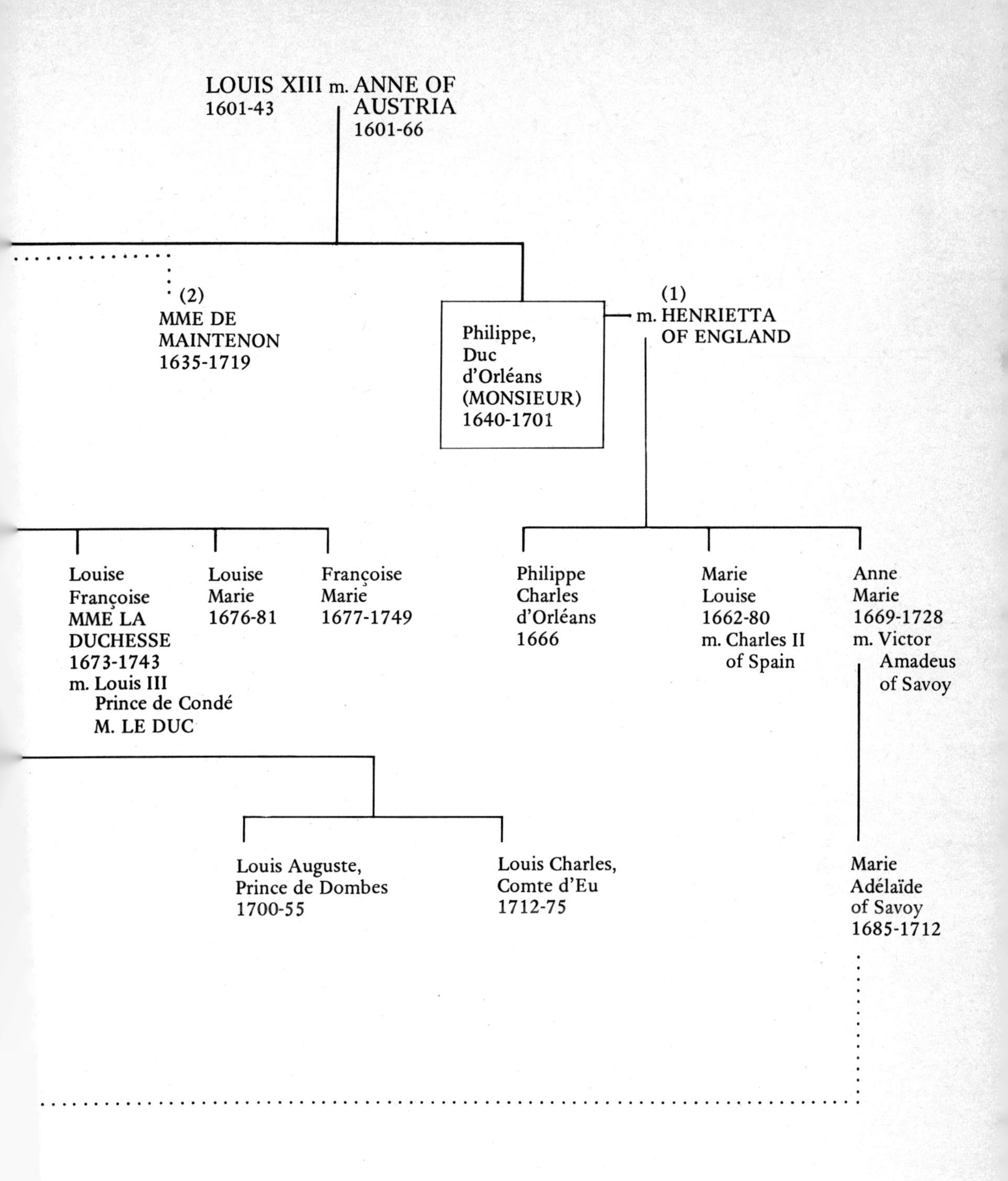

LOUIS XIII m. ANNE OF AUSTRIA
1601-43
1601-66
(2)
MME DE MAINTENON
1635-1719
Philippe, Duc d'Orléans (MONSIEUR)
1640-1701
(1)
m. HENRIETTA OF ENGLAND
Louise Françoise MME LA DUCHESSE
1673-1743
m. Louis III Prince de Condé M. LE DUC
Louise Marie
1676-81
Françoise Marie
1677-1749
Philippe Charles d'Orléans
1666
Marie Louise
1662-80
m. Charles II of Spain
Anne Marie
1669-1728
m. Victor Amadeus of Savoy
Louis Auguste, Prince de Dombes
1700-55
Louis Charles, Comte d'Eu
1712-75
Marie Adélaïde of Savoy
1685-1712

List of Illustrations

2 Louis XIV, *Photographie Bulloz*
3 Bust of Louis XIV, *Michael Holford Library*
10–11 Louis XIV, *The Mansell Collection*
12 Louis XIV, *Photographie Bulloz*
14 The infant Louis, *Photographie Giraudon*
15 Madame de Lansac, *Photographie Giraudon*
16 Louis XIII, sculptor JEAN WARIN, *Photographie Giraudon*
17 Anne of Austria, *Radio Times Hulton Picture Library*
18–19 Marriage of Louis XIII, *Photographie Giraudon*
22–23 Louis XIV, *The Mansell Collection*
25 Louis XIV, *The Mansell Collection*
26 Gaston d'Orléans, engraving from portrait by VAN DYCK, *Mary Evans Picture Library*
28 Duchesse de Longueville, artists BEAUBRUN BROTHERS, *Photographie Bulloz*
28–29 Barricade in Paris, *Photographie Bulloz*
32–33 Louis XIV, *The Mansell Collection*
34 Louis XIV as Jupiter, *Service de Documentation Photographique des Musées Nationaux*
36–37 Louis XIV at Fontainebleau, artist VAN DER MEULEN, *Alinari-Giraudon*
40–41 Louis XIV, *Photographie Bulloz*
45 Maria Teresa, *Museo del Prado*
46 Marriage of Louis XIV, *Photographie Bulloz*
48 Triumphal Arch, *Weidenfeld and Nicolson Archive*
54 Nicolas Fouquet, artist BOURDON, *Service de Documentation Photographique des Musées Nationaux*
57 Mazarin, artist PIERRE MIGNARD, *Photographie Bulloz*
57 Mazarin's nieces, *Photographie Bulloz*
58 Philippe d'Orléans, *Photographie Bulloz*
59 Duchesse d'Orléans, after PIERRE MIGNARD, *National Portrait Gallery*
60 Louis as a minor, artist PIERRE MIGNARD, *Photographie Giraudon*
61 Ceiling of Vaux-le-Vicomte, *Weidenfeld and Nicolson Archive*
61 Louis XIV, artist CHARLES LE BRUN, *Service de Documentation Photographique des Musées Nationaux*
62 Louise de La Vallière, artist J. NOCRET, *The Mansell Collection*
64–65 Equestrian statue of Louis XIV, sculptor BERNINI, *The Mansell Collection*
66 Vaux-le-Vicomte, builder LOUIS LE VAU, photographer EDWIN SMITH
69 Louis XIV, artist CHARLES LE BRUN, *Photographie Giraudon*
70 Charles Le Brun and Pierre Mignard, *Mary Evans Picture Library*
70–71 Louis XIV at tapestry works, *The Mansell Collection*
72 Monsieur, *Photographie Giraudon*
74 The Salon de la Guerre at Versailles, relief by ANTOINE COYSEVOX, *Michael Holford Library*
74–75 Versailles, artist JEAN-BAPTISTE MARTIN, *Photographie Bulloz*
76 André Le Nôtre, *The Mansell Collection*

76–77 The Marly Machine, *A. C. Cooper Limited*
77 La Fontaine de Flore, engraver LEPAUTRE, *La Bibliothèque Nationale (Archives M. Rieussec)*
77 Gardens at Versailles, photographer EDWIN SMITH
80 Louis XIV at tapestry works, *The Mansell Collection*
82–83 *Les Plaisirs de l'Ile Enchantée, John R. Freeman and Company Limited*
84 Versailles, *Roger Viollet Collection*
86–87 Royal family, *Photographie Bulloz*
90–91 Louis XIV playing billiards, *The Mansell Collection*
92–93 Louis XIV and Siamese Ambassadors, *British Museum*
94–95 Versailles, artist VAN DER MEULEN, *A. C. Cooper Limited*
98–99 The Academy of Science and Fine Arts, engraver SÉBASTIEN LE CLERC, *Photographie Bulloz*
100 Jean-Baptiste Colbert, artist LEFEBVRE, *Archives Photographiques*
102–103 The Invalides, builder JULES HARDOUIN-MANSARD, *A. C. Cooper Limited*
107 A merchant banker, *La Bibliothèque Nationale (Archives M. Rieussec)*
108 Lender and Borrower, *La Bibliothèque Nationale (Archives M. Rieussec)*
111 Marriage á la mode, *La Bibliothèque Nationale (Archives M. Rieussec)*
112 La Toilette, *La Bibliothèque Nationale (Archives M. Rieussec)*
115 Doctor, *La Bibliothèque Nationale (Archives M. Rieussec)*
116 Peasant woman, artist LOUIS LE NAIN, *Photographie Bulloz*
118 A countryman, *Roger Viollet Collection*
119 Peasant woman, *Roger Viollet Collection*
120–121 The baker's cart, artist MICHELIN, *Photographie Bulloz*
122 Illustration of a proverb, artist J. LAGNIER, *Roger Viollet Collection*
124–125 Scenes from Molière's plays, *Mary Evans Picture Library*
127 Marie de Rabutin-Chantal, Marquise de Sévigné, *Photographie Bulloz*
128 Blaise Pascal, artist DOMAT, *Photographie Bulloz*
129 Nicolas Boileau-Despréaux, artist HYACINTHE RIGAUD, *Photographie Bulloz*
130 Molière, artist PIERRE MIGNARD, *Photographie Bulloz*
133 Molière, *La Bibliothèque Nationale (Archives M. Rieussec)*
134–135 *La Malade Imaginaire, Photographie Bulloz*
136–137 Louis XIV and Molière, artist INGRES, *Photographie Bulloz*
137 *L'Ecole des Femmes, Photographie Bulloz*
138 Pierre Corneille, *The Mansell Collection*
141 Horace, *Roger Viollet Collection*
142 Frontispiece for works of Racine, designer CHARLES LE BRUN, *The Mansell Collection*
142 *Bérénice, Photographie Bulloz*
143 Jean Racine, *Photographie Bulloz*
145 *Esther, Roger Viollet Collection*
146 Tribute to Jean de La Fontaine, engraver JEAN-BAPTISTE OUDRY, *Roger Viollet Collection*
149 Jacques-Bénigne Bossuet, *Roger Viollet Collection*
151 François de Salignac de la Mothe-Fénelon, *Photographie Bulloz*
152 Jean de La Bruyère, *Photographie Bulloz*
154–155 Louis XIV entering Arras, artist VAN DER MEULEN, *Photographie Bulloz*
158–159 Louis XIV declaring war, *The Mansell Collection*
161 Louis XIV on horseback, *Photographie Giraudon*
165 Anne of Austria, *Radio Times Hulton Picture Library*
166 Madame de Montespan, *Photographie Bulloz*
169 Mlle de La Vallière, artist PIERRE MIGNARD, *Photographie Bulloz*

170–171 French and Italian actors, *Photographie Giraudon*
172 La Voisin, engraver CHASTEAU, *Roger Viollet Collection*
174–175 La Voisin and the Affair of the Poisons, *Photographie Giraudon*
176 The Marriage of *le Grand Dauphin,* *Roger Viollet Collection*
178–179 The insignia of royalty, *John R. Freeman and Company Limited*
180 The royal family relaxing, *Photographie Bulloz*
180 The Duc de Berry, artist VIVIEN, *Photographie Bulloz*
181 The Duc de Bourgogne, *The Mansell Collection*
181 The Duc d'Anjou, *Photographie Bulloz*
182 Mlle de la Vallière, artist LELY, *Photographie Bulloz*
183 Marquise de Montespan, *Photographie Giraudon*
184 Paul Scarron, *The Mansell Collection*
186 Mme de Maintenon, *Roger Viollet Collection*
187 Mme de Maintenon, *Photographie Bulloz*
188–189 Mme de Maintenon at Saint-Cyr, *Roger Viollet Collection*
192–193 Louis XIV, *Photographie Giraudon*
196 The King in Council, engraver JAN LUIKEN, *Photographie Giraudon*
198 William III, artist J. WYCK, *National Portrait Gallery*
199 Louis XIV in the trenches, *The Mansell Collection*
201 La Hogue, *The Mansell Collection*
202–203 *Le Grand Dauphin,* artist PIERRE MIGNARD, *Photographie Bulloz*
204 Duc d'Anjou declared King of Spain, *Roger Viollet Collection*
206–207 French cartoon, *Photographie Bulloz*
208 Popular art of the early eighteenth century, *British Museum*
210–211 The lying in state of Louis XIV, *Photographie Bulloz*
214–215 Convent of Port-Royal-des-Champs, *Photographie Giraudon*
212–213 An urn in the gardens of Versailles, photographer EDWIN SMITH
217 Louis XV, *John R. Freeman and Company Limited*
218 The Grand Monarch, artist VAN DER MEULEN, *Photographie Bulloz*
221 Louis XIV, *La Bibliothèque Nationale (Archives M. Rieussec)*
222 A triumphal arch, designer CLAUDE PERNAULT, *Mary Evans Picture Library*

Endpaper: Château de Versailles, vue prise de la Cour de Marbre, artist J.-B. MARTIN, *Photographie Giraudon*

Index

L XIV = Louis XIV

Acton, Lord:
quoted 13
Aix-la-Chapelle, Treaty of 156, 157
Anjou, Philippe, Duc d' (brother of L XIV) SEE Orléans, Philippe I, Duc de
Anjou, Philippe, Duc d' (Great-grandson of L XIV) SEE Philip V, King of Spain
Arnold, Matthew:
quoted 139
Aubigné, Agrippa d' 177
Augsburg, League of 197
Aumale, Mlle d':
quoted 191
mentioned 209
Austria, Anne of (mother of L XIV):
character 16
career 16–21, 25, 27, 30–1
piety 39, 42
and L XIV *10–11, 25, 46*
and Mazarin 21
death of 132, 164
mentioned 13, *17, 18–9,* 39, 43, 56, *86–7, 165*
Avaux, Félibien des:
quoted 156

Beauvais, Bishop of 21
Bérénice, L XIV inspires Racine to write 44
Bernini, Lorenzo *3, 64–5,* 79, 164
Boileau-Despréaux, Nicolas (*known* as Boileau):
assessed 130
mentioned *129,* 132, 142, 144, 147
Bolingbroke. Lord:
quoted 39
Bossuet, Jacques-Bénigne, Bishop of Meaux:
assessed 148
quoted 148, 195
mentioned 38, *149,* 153
Boulle, André-Charles 68
Bourgogne, Duc de (grandson of L XIV) 150, 174, *177–8, 181,* 200, 204, 207, 209
Broussel, Pierre 30

Cassini 107
Charlemagne 13
Charles II, King of England 26
Choisy, Abbé de:
quoted 194
Clement XI, Pope 200
Colbert, Jean-Baptiste:
character 61
career 101–110
assessed 106
mentioned 68, 73, 79, *100,* 117, 157, 162, 177, 219
Comédie-Française 139
Condé, Prince de (le Grand Condé) 30, 163, 174
Conseil, des Dépêches 53
d'état 53
des Finances 53
privé 53
Conti, Prince de 30
Corneille, Pierre:
career 140
assessed 140
mentioned 52, 55, *138,* 139, 144

Descartes, René 126
Droit, coutumier 104
écrit 104

Evelyn, John 38

Foucault, Nicolas-Joseph:
quoted 194
Fouquet, Nicolas:
character 55
career 55
arrest 61, 63
mentioned 42, *54,* 61, 67, 101, 147
Fronde 35, 42, 50, 55, 150, 219

the First 27, 30
the Second 30
Fronde des Princes 30, 31, 150

Gaulle, Charles de 156, 219
Godeau, Bishop 38
Gondi, Paul de (Cardinal de Retz) 30
Gramont, Duc de 44
Grimani:
quoted 162, 163

Hapsburg family 13, 16, 20
Hardouin-Mansard, Jules *102–3*, 168, 191, 219
Henri IV, King of France:
assessed 13
mentioned 38, 56, 177, 195
Henrietta (wife of Philippe d'Orléans) 56, *59*, *86–7*
Henrietta Maria, Queen of England (wife of Charles I) *86–7*

Innocent XIII, Pope 204
Inscription maritime 105

James II, King of England 197, 204
Jansenism 200, *214–5*

La Bruyère, Jean de:
career 150
assessed 153
quoted 97, 219
mentioned *152*, 219
La Fontaine, Jean de:
career 147
assessed 147, 148
mentioned 55, 126, 142, 146, 200
La Porte (*valet de Chambre* of L XIV):
quoted 24
La Reynie, Nicolas-Gabriel de 101
La Rochefoucauld, François VI, Duc de:
career 150
assessed 150
La Vallière, Louise de:
appearance 56, *62*, *182*
character 56, 164
love-affair with L XIV 56, 164, 167
enters convent 168, *169*
death of 168
mentioned 79, 185, 190
Land tax 55
Lansac, Mme de: *15*
Le Brun, Charles (artist to L XIV) *61*, 63, 67, 68, *69*, *70*, *142*, *158–9*, 164, 219
Le Nôtre, André (designer of gardens to L XIV) 68, 70, *76*, 79, 219, 222
Le Vau, Louis (architect to L XIV) *66*, 67, 79
Lionne, Hugues de 55, 174
Longueville, Duc de 30
Longueville, Duchesse de *28*, 31
Louis XIII, King of France (father of L XIV):
assessed 13
death of 20
mentioned 13, 14, *16*, *18–9*
Louis XIV, King of France:
birth 13
childhood *10–11*, *12*, *14*, *15*, 24, *60*
education 24, 43
appearance *2*, *3*, 6, 24, *22–3*, *25*, *32–3*, *34*, *36–7*, *40–1*, *61*, *64–5*, *69*, *70–1*, *80*, *82–3*, *86–7*, *90–1*, *92–3*, *134–5*, *136–7*, *154–5*, *158–9*, *161*, *178–9*, *180*, *196*, *199*, *204*, *218*, *221*
accomplishments of 39, 160–3
kingship and 38, 50–3
warlike instincts of 106, 156, 157
failings of 156–160, 194, 195
marriage of (to Maria Teresa) 44, 49
marriage of (to Mme de Maintenon) 185
love-affairs of 43, 56, 164–174, 177–191
death of 209–211, *210–11*
Versailles and 63, 67–97
assessed 25, 196, 197, 215–22
quoted 43, 44, 50, 51, 52, 156, 162, 163, 209, 216
Louis XV, King of France 174, 216, *217*, 220
Louis XVI, King of France 174, 220
Louis, *le Grand Dauphin* (son of L XIV) 50, *86–7*, *149*, 174, *176*, *202–3*, 207
Louvois, Michel Le Tellier, Marquis de 53, 101, 106, 157, 194
Louvre, Palais du 38, 67, 106
Lully, Jean-Baptiste 78, 137, 162, 191, 219

Maintenon, Françoise, Mme de,

formerly Mme Scarron (wife of L XIV):
appearance *186*, *187*, *188–9*, 190
character 177, 185
career 177–191
marriage to L XIV 185
death of 216
quoted 96, 206, 207
mentioned 144, 150, 194, 207, 209, 210, 220
Mancini, Marie:
described 43
L XIV in love with 43
L XIV abandons 43
Maria Teresa (wife of L XIV):
appearance *45*, 49, *154–5*
character 55, 56
marriage 44, *46*, 49
death of 177
mentioned *86–7*, 168, 174, 185
Marie Anne de Bourbon 225
Mazarin, Jules, Cardinal:
character 21, 50
career 20, 21, 27–31, 43, 44
appearance *25*, *46*, *57*
and Anne of Austria 21
death of 49
mentioned 35, 38, 39, 50, 53, 56, 61, 85, 101, 104, 132, 156, 162, 196
nieces of 44, *57*
Michelet, Jules 186, 221
Mignard, Pierre *57*, *59*, *60*, *70*, *130*, *169*, *202–3*
Molière (Jean-Baptiste Poquelin):
career 130–9
assessed 139, 142
mentioned 63, 79, 97, 130, *130*, *133*, *136–7*, 162, *170–1*, 200, 219
Montespan, Athénaïs, Marquise de:
appearance *166*, 167, *183*
character 167
career 167–174
love-affair with L XIV 167–174
and Affair of Poisons 173, 174
mentioned 79, 144, 177, 190, 220
Monvoisin, Catherine 173
Mothe-Fénelon, François de Salignac de la, Archbishop of Cambrai:
career 148, 150
assessed 150
quoted 200
mentioned *151*, 204
Motteville, Mme de:
quoted 21, 30, 39, 49

Navy 105
Nijmegen, Treaty of 157, 160

Orléans, Gaston, Duc d' (uncle of L XIV) 26, *26*, 31, 85
Orléans, Philippe I, Duc d' (brother of L XIV, Monsieur): *10–11*, *15*, 24, 27, 43, *46*, 49, 56, *58*, 72, 85, *86–7*, 89, *199*
Orléans, Philippe II, Duc d', the regent: 209, *217*, 220
Paris 101, 114–19
Parlement (of Paris) 13, 20, 27, 29, 30, 31, 35, 42, 96
Pascal, Blaise:
assessed 129
mentioned *128*, 200
Pays, d'election 104
d'etat 104
Péréfixe, Hardouin de Beaumont de (tutor of L XIV) 24, 38, 136
Petit, M. 73
Philip IV, King of Spain 44, 156
Philip V, King of Spain (Duc d'Anjou): 177, *181*, *204*, 205, 207
Port-Royal, Paris, convent of *214–15*
Port-Royal-des-champs, Versailles, convent of *214–15*
Pyrenees, Treaty of the 44, 49, 156

Quietism 200, 204

Racine, Jean:
career 140, 142
assessed 144, 147
mentioned 130, 139, *143*, 144, 191, 219
Ravaillac 24
Regency of L XIV 16, 20, 27, 31
Revolution 104, 220, 221
Richelieu, Armand du Plessis, Cardinal 20, 21, 39, 104, 130, 196
Roemer 107
Ryswick, Treaty of 204

Saint-Cyr 144, *188–9*, 191, 216

Saint-Maurice, Marquis de:
quoted 156, 157
Saint-Simon, Louis de Rouvroy, Duc de:
quoted 73, 85, 88, 89, 163, 195, 199, 205, 216
Scarron, Paul 177, *184*, 185
Scarron, Mme Paul (*see also* Maintenon, Mme de) 49, 79, 177
Sévigné, Mme de:
quoted 56, 73, 126, 148, 168, 173, 174, 177, 184
mentioned 109, 126, *127*
Spanish Succession, War of the 205

Talon, Omer 38
Third Estate 109
Thirty Years' War 29, 42
Turenne, Maréchal de 31, 35

Urban VIII, Pope 20
Utrecht, Treaty of 207

Vaux-le-Vicomte *61*, 63, *66*, 67, 70
Versailles, Château de:
origins of 63, 67
L XIV builds 67, 71, 73
described 68, *74*, *74–5*, *77*, *82*–3, *84*, *94–5*, *180*

Visconti, Primi:
quoted 73, 160, 164, 197
Voltaire (François-Marie Arouet) 79, 115, 216, 222

William III, King of England 197, *198*, 204